THE WOUNDE

EVANGELICALS IN EX

EVANGELICALS IN EXILE

WRESTLING WITH THEOLOGY
AND THE UNCONSCIOUS

Alistair Ross

DARTON · LONGMAN + TODD

First published in 1997 by
Darton, Longman and Todd Ltd
1 Spencer Court
140–142 Wandsworth High Street
London SW18 4JJ

ISBN 0–232–52218–9

A catalogue record for this book is available
from the British Library.

The Scripture quotations in this publication are taken from
the New International Version of the Bible published by
Hodder and Stoughton Ltd.

Phototypeset by Intype London Ltd
Printed and bound in Great Britain by
Redwood Books, Trowbridge, Wiltshire

CONTENTS

FOREWORD

The 'Wounded Pilgrim' series was originally conceived as a response to the Churches' call for a decade of evangelism or evangelisation. Those writers who have contributed to the series have done so not in a spirit of triumphalism but from a poignant awareness of their vulnerability. They have drawn on the experience of their own often painful and desperate struggle to hold on to God in the face of psychological and emotional anguish and in many instances, of the uncomprehending or hostile responses of their co-religionists. As editor of the series it has been my privilege to stand alongside a group of writers who have risked telling it as it is and who have not drawn back from the self-exploration and self-exposure which such a commitment to truth inevitably involves. It is my conviction that it is precisely such transparency with its openness and ready acknowledgement of doubt, uncertainty or even despair that can touch the hearts and minds of those who at the close of the millennium yearn for meaning and affirmation as our materialistic society blunders on to it knows not where.

Alistair Ross is a worthy recruit to the ranks of the wounded pilgrims. He is a Baptist minister trained in and nourished by the evangelical tradition with its confident assertion of salvation and its direct and authoritative proclamation of the gospel. In his personal and professional life, however, he has experienced the shadow side of such apparent confidence and certainty. He has been on the receiving end of a scarcely veiled judgementalism which seeks to measure evangelical purity and he has encountered the narrowness of mind by which some define spirituality in the blinkered terms of the evangelical world. His experience and training as a group therapist and analytical counsellor have further intensified both his inner conflict and the pain of falling victim to the dysfunctional life of some institutional Churches. He has been brought to the very edge of the abyss by his encounter with the apparent refusal of those in leadership positions to face psychological reality and to acknowledge its relevance to the life of the Christian community and to the living out of relationships in love. Bruised and battered by his several experiences, he has known the desolation of spiritual exile but in this often lonely place he has found the friends, the therapists and the clients who have enabled him to move to the space (a beloved metaphor) where he can be himself with all his splits and paradoxes. It is a space where he is infinitely more vulnerable than he would ever be as the apparently self-confident minister exercising the somewhat macho style of leadership which can characterise some evangelical pastors whose faith brooks no doubt and whose hot line to God ensures a ready answer to every dilemma.

Alistair knows that his journey continues but for the moment he is glad to have arrived at a resting place where he experiences the exhilaration of living life more fully and of welcoming the challenges of psychological and spiritual encounter with himself, with others and with God. What is more he desires still to affirm his evangelical identity even if others within the 'family' regard him uneasily. It is my hope that his tenacity in trusting his own experience and his fearless confrontation with psychological and emotional pain and confusion will act as a reassuring beacon for those who know in the depths of their being that they must undertake a similar journey but are fearful that they will lose God on the way. This book provides further compelling evidence that it is in the very pain and confusion that God is often to be found if we can but believe that we are the beloved of the Creator whose only desire is that we shall be free to be ourselves in his company.

BRIAN THORNE
Norwich 1997

INTRODUCTION

The Evangelical Church with its emphasis on biblical authority, the person of Jesus Christ – especially the centrality of his death and resurrection – the experience of conversion and the mission to save the world has experienced a remarkable renaissance in the last two decades.[1] That same Church is now undergoing a revolution. Those within this world are questioning whether they are post-evangelical, radical evangelical or, as I shall explore in this book, evangelicals that other evangelicals are very uncomfortable with and would rather see exiled in some remote island like Napoleon on Elba or in some fortress island prison like Alcatraz. Yet why is asking questions perceived to be so dangerous? I am an evangelical and I am passionate about living my life, asking my questions, exploring new ideas and reaching out to hurting people with love. Gillian Rose has called her reflections on life's experiences, *Love's Work*. Drawing on Jewish, Christian and philosophical aspects of her self, she writes and speaks for me when she says,

> However satisfying writing is – that mix of discipline and miracle, which leaves you in control, even when what appears on the page has emerged from regions beyond your control – it is a very poor substitute for the joy and agony of loving...To lose this is the greatest loss, a loss for which there is no consolation. There can only be that twin passion – the passion of faith.[2]

Those themes of love, loss, the unconscious, twinness, and faith resonate throughout my reflections on some of life's experiences as a minister of religion and counsellor. I have explored my

1

Christian faith (originally from an evangelical perspective but now on the borders, but still within that faith description) and my Christian calling (to bring wholeness to as many people as possible, working from within the church) from theological and psychological perspectives. I have ventured and risked offering a way of exploring my story by identifying some of the psycho-theological dynamics that I see at work in me, other individuals and various types of institution. My psychological quest has drawn me to the core of people's lives – meeting, experiencing, describing, identifying and being with other persons. My theological quest has been shaped by conversion, and re-meeting God (paradoxically more simple and complex) in myself, others, the Word of God and the Church.

This book is about loving and faith and one of the joyful aspects of writing is the fresh discovery of many that have loved me and whom I have tried to love in return. This story could not have been written without them and all they have given to me. It is a yet to be completed story in which I can give heartfelt thanks for Judy, Hannah and Toby, my parents, brothers and sisters, Judy's parents and sisters. For a colourful and intricate kaleidoscope of friends – Keith, Mike, Jeannie, Malcolm, Margaret, Pat, Andy, Paul, Dave and Cathy, Jonathan, Ruth and Angie – all of whom have reflected back to me aspects of myself as they view me. For various church communities in London, Kent and Birmingham where I have served and endeavoured to put theory into practice and not always succeeded. For past therapists and supervisors, especially Tony and Michael, who have enabled me to continue in this vital therapeutic task in a way that more authentically offers 'me' to clients. For many clients, especially Rachel (who contributes Chapter 7) whose risk-taking and life-affirming friendship fills me with admiration.

This story has been written with passion, a passion I hope the reader will come to share through engaging with this tale. My wish is that we might be better able to recognise those divergent yet life-affirming strands of self and experience, the risks of love and faith, that God calls us to share.

1

FAMILY MATTERS

Seven months after my parents married, I was born. The birth was as eventful as the wedding night conception, not so much for my parents as for me. During a counselling course I attended, time was given to a guided meditation concerning life in the womb. In the darkened room, lit with a candle, the following images and feelings arrived unexpectedly, like snow descending on a cold autumn day. I can only describe it this way. In the warm, inky darkness there reverberated an echo. Another echo, another heartbeat, not my own. I was not alone. From the moment of conception there have been two, not one. Two beings competing for space, sustenance, acceptance and love. Two beings sharing intimacy and belonging.

Our removal from one 'safe' world to an unknown other, happened sooner than expected. My twin was born in the early hours of 6 June 1957 and I followed ten minutes later, two months premature at 'Homelands', a Salvation Army nursing home in Glasgow. The arrival of two instead of one was a complete surprise and shock for my parents. At birth my mother asked the midwife if it was a boy or a girl and was told it was a girl. My mother replied, 'That's a shame. Jim [my father] wanted a boy', only to be told, 'Let's wait and see what the next one is.' This was the first inkling that twins were to be born. Elizabeth weighed just over 3lbs and I weighed just over 4lbs. My mother's apocryphal tale is that we were so small we were put to sleep in a shoe box. Survival, in those days when an incubator was as high tech as one got, was not guaranteed. It was greatly helped by the matron and assistant matron who took it in turns to give us hourly feeds of an ounce

3

of milk through a drip, via a tube, into the stomach. Although my mother visited every day, it was six weeks before I, now named James Alistair, was able to come home and seven weeks before Elizabeth Ann could follow.

As a pastoral theologian and psychodynamic counsellor with a particular interest in Frank Lake and Donald Winnicott,[1] I often wonder about those early weeks and months, both in the womb and out of it. When does one's embryonic personality begin? What nurtures, develops, hinders or limits one's personality? How does 'being' begin and become? The broader and deeper the knowledge I acquire, the greater the curiosity I experience about something that is part of me, that seems so tantalisingly close and yet remains so distant. What I do know is that with two, there is always a competitor, a rival, another mouth crying to be fed, another demanding time, energy and attention from the warm, sustaining object that one gradually learns to identify as mother.

I am also aware of the sense of my father's absence. He was not there at the birth as few, if any, men were present at birth in those days. It was however a powerful symbol of experience in later life, when I perceived him there but somehow absent. This feeling became clear to me when I saw him with my own son, Toby. My father doesn't appear to possess an ability to 'be' with children. Toby sat on his knee, as he does with his other granddad and wanted his grandfather, known as 'Jimbo', to play with him. The stiff limbs, the inability to relax, the lack of a capacity to play, the sheer sense of distance brought memories and emotions flooding back like waves crashing against a sea wall. Seeing my son with my father enabled me to see 'me' as a boy. While my father was occasionally physically absent from my childhood, when he was there he seemed to be emotionally absent. When he did give of himself, even this still needed to be shared, not just with my twin, but with the other four children that followed in rapid succession, including another set of twins, although one of these was stillborn.

Reflecting back on my childhood and exploring this in therapy with a male, psychodynamically trained and eclectic therapist I discovered four themes emerging that contain a particular force or life to them. These are themes of conflict and competition, loss, risk-taking and a search for belonging. As I tell my story, I cannot artificially separate out these elements, as they are inextricably woven together.

Not surprisingly I was in conflict with my twin sister, Elizabeth. Unless one has been a twin or studied twins it is difficult to describe the mixed feelings and emotions of both intimacy and rivalry that are provoked by the continual presence of another. As fraternal twins, and therefore less likely to face the problems some people have in giving identical twins a distinct identity, we still experienced a rivalry between us. The fragmentary memories of childhood remind me of our ability to annoy each other. I would pretend I had sweets when she didn't, and she would insist that she should have first choice as she was the eldest. Yet there was an intimacy, too. On one occasion Elizabeth tripped in the classroom and caught her lip on a sharp metal corner of a desk. This tore her lip and she had to be taken to hospital for stitches to be inserted, although in herself she was fine. I was in the same class, although at a different desk and suddenly I began to shiver, feel nauseous and was subsequently taken home from school as I was experiencing all the symptoms of shock. By right she should have been experiencing all these symptoms but in fact was well enough to want to go back to school.

My memories of school are dominated by this small school in Bonnyrigg, a village about twelve miles outside Edinburgh. We had moved from our tenement flat in Glasgow to a new overspill estate built on the edge of this village. My feelings, as an adult, about this school are ones of Dickensian horror. The teacher obviously thought that these 'outsiders' in their smart new school uniforms, that contrasted with the clothes of the other village children, needed to be 'put in their place'. This became obvious when in the first week at school I lost my spelling book. Each night we were given a list of words to learn, that we were tested on the following day. In the chaos of moving to a new house and the turmoil caused by two brothers and a sister (another was to arrive later), losing a book was an easy thing to do. Every day I turned up at school without my spelling book I was given the 'strap'. This was a thick, leather band that was used to hit the hand or the bottom of the unfortunate victim. Every day I did not have my spelling book I was given another stroke. Fortunately by the fourth day (after the number of beatings with the strap had gone up to three) I found it, yet until then I had endured the pain and public humiliation of standing in front of the whole class to be hit. It felt so unfair and so inflexible. Did this teacher, a powerful authority figure, not understand that things genuinely get lost? There was a threat and rigidity about that place that, unconsciously, I was never comfortable with. Yet my unconscious was clearly at work as during this time I experienced two recurring and vivid nightmares. I was either climbing up an endless series of ladders and never arriving at the unknown but desired destination or, more frighteningly, I experienced the sensation of falling down an unending tunnel like some dark mine shaft, similar to those which were to be found in the local disused pit workings.

Every Friday the class were given a test and, depending on the result, we were moved to a desk that indicated how well or badly we had done. I was always in the bottom row, while Elizabeth was always in the top row. The lesson I learnt in this bleak, cold school was that one needed to conform if one was to survive. Yet I have always found a rigid conformity in any sphere something that I react against. I want space and freedom in order to discover me and this was certainly not the place in which such a discovery was encouraged. It did, however, sow the seeds of a rich, fantastic imagination that now finds expression in my creative thinking and writing.

Life, dominated by school, was not all bad. There were exceptions and the most vivid was a visit to London with my father. Dressed in my Sunday best, a Ross tartan kilt complete with sporran, I left Edinburgh on board the 'Flying Scotsman' (a diesel train named after the original steam locomotive), London bound. It was the stuff of dreams. After arriving at Kings Cross station, we walked for what seemed like miles, until my father found a hotel that would provide bed and breakfast for ten shillings instead of twelve shillings and sixpence. Interestingly, my father's recollection of this, is that many of the hotels were suspicious of a man and a boy on their own and it took some time to find one that would take us. London at night is a glamorous place for a seven year old. We gazed at the bright lights of Piccadilly Circus and joined the crowds waiting to see the arrival of someone outside a cinema. A policeman noticed that all I could see was a forest of legs and made way for me to stand next to him at the front of the crowd. A large black limousine glided to a halt outside and out climbed the Queen, attending a Royal film premiere. The silk dress, the fur stole and the twinkling diamonds of her tiara, merged with the cheers and applause of the crowd as I was overwhelmed by one of those rare but awesome moments when fantasy becomes reality and knowledge becomes truth. Yet in it all there is the memory of the kindness of the policeman. That long remembered, glittering occasion had its roots in the 'down to earthness' of being noticed and of someone doing something 'special' just for me.

The first cultural shock occurred when I wanted to go to the toilet. In our house, full of children as it was, if someone was in the toilet and the door was locked, we would shout out 'It's busy'. I tried and tried to get into the toilet in the hotel and eventually a plump, middle-aged man came out, smiled at this little boy in a kilt, and went back to his breakfast. I was mystified. If he had been in there all that time, why hadn't he shouted out? The rest of the weekend I cannot remember other than the fact that it was one of those special occasions when I had my dad to myself and we were doing something together. It is one of those 'special' memories of childhood for that very reason.

Bonnyrigg was the place where I discovered the joy and pain of friendship. I made my first friend outside the family. Until now the presence of a twin made such a person, a friend, unnecessary. All I can remember now was his surname, Johnson. It was with Johnson, I first discovered my ability to tell stories. I told him all about a golden eagle that we kept in the loft, that came out at night to hunt sheep, dogs and other animals. I was a bit taken aback when he asked to see it. I hurriedly invented the excuse that it was far too fierce to be seen by a little boy, ignoring the obvious problem that I too was a little boy. When his dad asked to see it, I knew the game was up. The other adventure that Johnson and I took part in was going to the 'pits'. This was a journey fraught with fear and excitement. It meant sneaking past the Police Constable's house, climbing over a fence and sliding down an embankment onto a railway line. Here we would wait for the telltale rumble of an approaching train and rush to put a rock on the line, or if we were feeling rich, a large copper penny. The train would 'hoot', we would cheer and the rock would crumble or the penny get bent and taken home as a souvenir. Then we would walk down the track until just before the signal-box where we would crawl through a cornfield, to avoid being seen. This would take us into a track leading to a disused coal-mine, where we would wander around, oblivious to the huge dangers of sunken shafts, unstable ground and buildings in a state of collapse. Yet it was freedom, risk, and excitement of the highest order. I have always been a risk taker and its roots go back to this early age of six.

The pain of friendship is often, but not exclusively, in the parting. My father's job moved to Bristol, so we moved. This pattern of moving and leaving friends behind was to happen again and again. Life in Bristol (Staple Hill to be precise) was somewhat different as we now moved to the first home my parents owned, a modern semi-detached house in a road of traditional stone terraced houses. We thought our neighbours exotic as he was the member of a rock group and she used to sunbathe topless in the back garden, a very risqué thing to do in 1965. The so-called 'Swinging Sixties' are an inaccurate cultural memory of ordinary suburban life.

School was a revelation. The buildings were modern rather than Victorian and the lessons were not strict at all. No strap (my faithful companion through school in Bonnyrigg), no spelling tests and no weekly ritual of being made aware that one was in the bottom section of the class. By the end of the term we had swapped places. I moved to the top of the class and Elizabeth moved to the bottom. Obviously she needed a very structured environment and I needed the freedom. This dual experience of early schooling has, I think, nurtured a dual aspect of my character – which is both an ability to be conformist but a desire to be non-conformist. There is in me a confidence that means I don't need to feel I conform in order to be accepted, and yet at times I still crave acceptance. In some ways this is a characteristic of a 'favourite' child.[2] Elizabeth and I agree that she retained the position of favourite twin until early adolescence when it passed to me.

The real discovery of this period was not so much school as Sunday school. Next to the school we went to, there was a little hall where on Sunday afternoons two elderly spinster sisters, complete with grey hair put up in 'buns', taught a Sunday school. My parents loved it, as it gave them peace and quiet, as all five of us would walk there and back on our own. We loved it, as we were given sweets afterwards (still a rare commodity in our home). The Misses Merrick, coming from a strict Brethren background, dutifully taught us stories from the Bible and at the age of eight, I had a clear understanding of Jesus' love for me. My own experiences of injustice and not being listened to found a champion in Jesus. My other hero was Martin Luther. This unlikely choice came about because of winning a prize at the Sunday school for attendance. The prize was a children's book about Martin Luther. His life read like the most exciting adventure story where good triumphed over evil. I wanted to be like Martin Luther, without knowing why or having any possible idea about how this could come about.

My best friend this time was Stephen Price. Together we went 'scrumping' for apples in people's gardens, raided the skips of rubbish at the warehouse of the Cox's cabinet company and raced round the back alleys on our bicycles. I always preferred it when he came to our house to play as his father was a dog handler for the police and kept a huge Alsatian in their garden, that frightened me to death. This time the loss came about not because we moved but because Stephen was a year older than me. He went to secondary school and didn't want to play with a kid still at junior school anymore. Before I made it to secondary school in Bristol, we moved again, this time to Yeovil in Somerset.

I regard my time at Yeovil Boys School, a grammar school, as the happiest period in my entire schooling. The reason for this was that I could start on equal terms with everyone else. I was not the new boy, trying to fit in with all the others; we were all new boys trying to fit in with each other. This came as a huge, warm, welcome relief, like some unexpected good news. They were as keen to be my friends as I was to be theirs. We shared the bewildering confusion of navigating our way around a vast collection of rooms and buildings that were now school. Gone was the safety, security and smallness of our former junior schools. We encountered 'prefects' who told us off for running, walking down the main drive, or not wearing our caps. With their powers of detention, I was soon in trouble. I had put a stink bomb inside a boy's pencil case that was set off when he opened it in class. I was made to stay after school and told to write a hundred words on 'the artistic merit of the nude'. I duly wrote my hundred words which, when handed in, sent the prefects into spasms of uncontrollable laughter. The title of the essay had been given verbally and not having seen the word written before, I had spelt it 'newd'. My inability to spell aside, I continued my story telling. The geography teacher had asked us to write an essay about the importance of oil in the Middle East. I had never heard the word essay before, so I wrote an adventure story about spies trying to sabotage oil pipelines in Saudi Arabia and ruining their economy. This was read out to the amusement of the class, though not in a way in which I was embarrassed. This was still a relatively new experience for me – to be approved of by a teacher in a way that gave me a certain 'character' and made me stand out from the crowd.

This school was an exciting place. I had my own best friend, Jeremy Sutcliffe (known as 'Sooty'), and I represented the school in rugby, cross-country and athletics. I was naturally sporting, gaining the Amateur Athletic Association's 'Five Star' Gold Award for under-thirteens when I was eleven. Following in my father's footsteps, I joined the Boys' Brigade (a Christian-based, uniformed boys' organisation). They also arranged many sporting activities, where I excelled. One year on sports day at the annual camp for the whole battalion (the counties of Somerset and Dorset), I won the marathon (a cross-country race), as well as the 100, 200, 400, 800 metres races and came fourth in the 1500 metres. I was rather tired by then as it was the last race that day. The reality was that I was a good, but not exceptional, athlete and not up against any real opposition.

Family life, with two brothers and two sisters, was a competitive affair. In order to gain attention each one of us had carved out a special place or staked a claim to be or do something more distinctive or better than anyone else. Elizabeth declared that she was the eldest and this gave her the right to be bossy. As well as this she was the smallest girl in her school which gave her a certain character. I was the sporty one and that was all that seemed to matter. David (two years younger) was reckoned by my parents to be the clever one. He was also the favourite. The universal lesson of Joseph's coat of many colours continually needs to be heeded (Genesis 37). It may be a bicycle rather than a coat but the effect on the rest of the brothers and sisters is profound. Kenneth (four years younger) was, to use my mother's words, 'the difficult one'. If ever there was a born scapegoat (a subject I will explore later) it was Kenneth, a fact seized on by the rest of us. Last, but not least, was Margaret (six years younger) who had been born when we were in Bonnyrigg, and as the 'baby' of the family was always able to get away with anything.

It is only now as an adult that I can see how my father, while still being there, somehow opted out of family life, leaving my mother in charge. I can see now that, whether she was aware of it or not, she always had a favourite and much of the family dynamics revolved around who was currently at the top of the chart. In fact to this day we, the children, now as adults, keep an eye on who is on the move up and who is on the way down. It is common for one or other of my brothers or sisters to ring up and say, 'Alistair, you're definitely at the bottom' and relate some incident where a comment has been made, indicating the current lie of the land. I am sure, knowing the little I do about my mother's childhood, that her rejection by her mother, in favour of her brother, left in her a need to have someone that would be special to her. Ironically it perpetuated the very thing she found so hard to bear herself.

Of all the places I had lived, Yeovil was where I felt I belonged. The school and the Boys' Brigade provided the outlets for my sporting and other activities (I also played chess for the school and was a treble in the school choir). Sooty and I saw each other in the holidays as well as at school, so everything was great. Well not quite. It was also through some 'friends' at school that I learnt to shoplift. A gang was started whose initiation rite was to steal a

11

wooden puzzle (costing two and sixpence) from the stand next to the cashier in W.H. Smith's. It was a bit of a laugh until one day several boys in school uniform were seen stealing and the Head was alerted. He began an internal enquiry that so frightened me that I stopped forthwith and the gang disbanded.

When we moved again, I felt the loss deeply, like a subterranean ache, yet I did not possess the emotional vocabulary to express it. This also occurred at a time when communication with my father became even more distant. His limited ability to relate to children became a silence as I passed into adolescence. The sense of belonging that I had created was smashed like some fragile ship pounded by the waves on to a rocky headland and it was to a place with rocky headlands that we moved.

2

FINDING FAITH

My family moved to Weston-super-Mare, a seaside resort that rarely sees the sea. The golden sand which appears on all the picture postcards, is nothing but a thin mineral veneer disguising Severn estuary mud. Weather-beaten hotels recall a golden yester-year. The grammar school which I attended was a similarly shabby, genteel, retired affair lacking the vibrancy, life, money, facilities, and quality teaching staff of my former school. All the things I loved doing were gone. Now thirteen, I was too old for a choir, had lost interest in chess, failed to enjoy rugby the way I once did and was told that the school didn't organise athletics matches as my previous school had done. All that remained was cross-country through the sand-dunes and mud flats of Uphill. The sense of loss, which I now see so clearly, is a key issue that clients raise with me repeatedly in counselling. Perhaps arising from this early experience of loss and others that were to follow, I have developed an instinct that sees loss in others the way X-rays reveal one's bones.

. I was unhappy but buried such feelings and got on with living. I was soon to discover a fundamental principle of counselling and psychotherapy, that powerful feelings and emotions do not stay buried. They have an uncomfortable proclivity towards resurrection. There were signs that all was not well in that I began shoplifting again (and, so he tells me, taught my brother as well). This was not major criminal activity, but my collection of football stickers made amazing progress. It came to a halt when my parents became suspicious and asked some direct questions. Why had I started this again? For the challenge, the adrenaline? It certainly wasn't to impress a group or belong to a gang. Looking back, I realise it was to get some attention. I wanted someone to see through the superficial 'settling well' which I showed to the world. Either my parents were more concerned about my younger brothers and sister, or I hid and repressed my real feelings more skilfully than I realised.

One element of continuity, which was in fact the cradle of a life-changing experience, was the discovery of another Boys' Brigade company, part of Milton Baptist Church. This was the first time we had been to a church that was evangelical in its theology. I threw myself into both the Boys' Brigade and the Young People's Group. My father became an officer in the same company and my parents began to attend church regularly. We had attended before but not with the same degree of commitment that now developed. There was about the church a sense of family and belonging that appealed to me. The YP was a lively group who enjoyed life, where an adolescent could feel free from parental control. At the age of fourteen, I decided to become a Christian which sounds very final and deterministic; in fact, it 'just happened'. The moment of revelation occurred while I was sitting in church listening to a talk based on Ernest Gordon's book *Miracle on the River Kwai*.[1] This described how Christians coped in the atrocious and brutal conditions of a Japanese POW camp, but were still able to show love to the Japanese who had so badly mistreated them. As well as appealing to my heroic imagination, it pointed to a quality of life that I wanted. I knew I could not find those resources within me. Then it dawned on me that being a Christian wasn't really about being a big, heroic, tough figure, it was about admitting that we are far from perfect. I knew I was far from perfect, the shoplifting episode was still alive in my conscience. Suddenly my need and God's benevolent gift in Christ fitted together, like two interlocking pieces of a yet to be solved puzzle. Ever since the age of eight through attending a Sunday school, I had known that Christ had died for people's sin, but until now I had been unaware that it was also for mine. I asked God to become real in my life. Nothing felt any different. There were no angel choirs singing hallelujahs, no Damascus road experience, no dramatic life-threatening encounter like Luther's, no altered state of consciousness, but there was a sense of peace that just grew and grew, like budding leaves on a tree in spring. I had become a Christian and to this day I thank God for my conversion and this life-changing experience of eternity in the present moment.

However, as time has gone on and as I have discovered more about the way people work and what motivates them, I realise that other powerful, psychological influences were at work. I desperately wanted to belong. I did belong in a family, with parents who loved me, even though my father could not articulate this. Yet I wanted to belong in my own right, as 'me'. Perhaps I saw in God just a glimpse of a Father who could love unconditionally,[2] but my primary focus of faith was on Jesus. I knew I was on safer ground with him as I have always been struck, even from my very first reading of the Gospels, by his acceptance of others as they really were. Importantly for me there were other people in the church, especially the YP leaders, who claimed to be Christians and who did demonstrate a love and acceptance of others that was more than a superficial 'niceness' brought about by regular church-going. I felt I belonged in the YP as 'me', whereas school was always about fitting in with others on their terms.

I look back on this as my first discovery that the language and experience of faith do not always match each other. There is always the danger of a split or unrelatedness between the two, an issue we will return to at a later stage. While this conversion experience was authentic and in Luther's words 'I felt myself to be reborn and to have gone through open doors into paradise,'[3] it was not 'the truth, the whole truth and nothing but the truth' for my view of God was very limited.[4] The God I had heard about and experienced in church was monochrome. The primary foci were Jesus Christ, understood in very human terms from the Gospels, and the all-powerful Almighty God, as opposed to God the Father, from the Old Testament. Passing reference was made to the Holy Ghost, which I envisaged as some benign, disembodied force rather like a white, floating tablecloth, but who was essentially absent apart from occasional guest appearances like a Hollywood celebrity being interviewed on a chat-show to promote his or her latest film. My theological understanding was

summed up by a then contemporary song written by the pioneering Christian rock musician Larry Norman (too rock and roll
for Christians and too Christian for the rockers and rollers!) called
'The Outlaw'.

> some say He was an outlaw, that He roamed across the land
> with a band of unschooled ruffians and a few old fishermen
> no one knew just where He came from or exactly what He'd
> done
> but they say it must be something bad that kept Him on the
> run
>
> some say He was a poet that He'd stand upon the hill
> and His voice could calm an angry crowd or make the waves
> stand still
> that He spoke in many parables that few could understand
> but the people sat for hours just to listen to this man
>
> some say He was a sorcerer a man of mystery
> He could walk upon the water He could make a blind man
> see that He conjured wine at weddings and did tricks with
> fish and bread
> that He talked about being born again and raised people from
> the dead
>
> some say a politician who spoke of being free
> He was followed by the masses on the shores of Galilee
> He spoke out against corruption and He bowed to no decree
> and they feared His strength and power so they nailed Him to
> a tree
>
> some say He was the Son of God, a man above all men
> but He came to be a servant and to set us free from sin
> and that's who I believe He was 'cause that's who I believe
> and I think we should get ready 'cause it's time for us to leave[5]

It is only as I write this that I have discovered that Larry Norman's
experience of a father was remarkably similar to mine. He writes,
'I understood that God was Jesus' Father, but did not realise that
He was also *my* Father and loved *me* personally.'[6]

I say this was the teaching I 'heard' because my lack of relationship with my father undoubtedly influenced the way I could perceive or not perceive God as Father. The images I had of God were of a remote awesome being who asked his followers to make the most unfair sacrifices, like Abraham's offering of Isaac in Genesis 22. Rather than get to know this God, I stayed with Jesus; at least I felt that I could understand him and believed that he understood me. This encounter with Jesus was much more than a meeting of a genuine psychological need, caricatured by Freud as an infantile wish fulfilment for a father expounded in his *Future of an Illusion*.[7] Yet it was less than a mature theological understanding of a spiritual reality. In order for this seed-like faith to grow, it needed nurturing.

The experience of conversion, however, did not improve life's circumstances. The disruption of changing schools was compounded a year later by the fact that the grammar school merged with the girls' grammar next door and a secondary modern school a mile down the road. Broadoak Comprehensive School's first year was one of rivalry, fragmentation, fear and excitement. The boys and girls from the secondary modern, who were much more streetwise than we, set the culture of the school. You either fitted in with them or were written off as a snob, a poof or a wanker. Their power, which made many of us from the grammar school envious, lay in their ability to talk and relate with people of the opposite sex. Coming from a single sex school, yet possessing a body complete with its fair share of newly manufactured hormones, I was both fascinated and fearful of these delightful, dream-inspiring, fantasy creatures called 'women'. The trouble was that the likes of me didn't stand any chance against the competition of the secondary modern boys. All we could do was look on enviously from a distance. The YP group provided an environment where it was much easier to mix with girls, without the competition or pressures found at school. I learnt how to talk to them and form relationships, even attaining the coveted status of 'going out' with a few. My real education in relationships however lay elsewhere.

The Seaview Hotel was hardly the Ritz. This formerly grand sandstone seafront hotel was owned by Mrs Price, a well-built

Welsh matriarch, who wore a fistful of diamonds and used to keep the takings in cash in her large handbag. My manipulation of the truth in saying that I had worked as a waiter, was conveniently overlooked by Mrs Price, and I started work the next day. It soon became apparent to all that I had never 'waited' before, so I was allowed to practise by serving Mrs Price's ten-year-old son. Every day he ordered the same lunch – breaded plaice, chips and peas – which he then drowned in a tidal wave of tomato sauce. As I whisked away the dinner plate from the kitchen hot-plate the plaice remained stationary suspended in mid air like some miniature Harrier jump-jet, before crashing to the floor. Bill, the duty chef (a tattooed, long-haired Hell's Angel), calmly picked it up from the floor, pieced it together on the plate, covered it with the regulation tomato sauce and sent me out into the dining room to serve the manageress's son.

The staff I encountered at the hotel educated me in the facts of life. Not sex, but the harsh reality of lives broken and exploited by relationships in which sex was a mere transaction, something to be used and traded. No television soap-opera or Hollywood mini-series could credibly contain such an unlikely and diverse group of characters. The 'cast' included: Glen, the head waiter who minced around in Scholl sandals, sported lacquered hair and spoke with an affected voice (that he was a homosexual, a fact uncovered by Bill during one of his regular forays into the hotel dustbins in search of discarded letters, surprised no one); Karin, a young Hungarian student who obtained British nationality through a marriage of convenience to Glen; Ted and Mary, who took me drinking to celebrate my first week's work which resulted in my first experience of drunkenness and an empty pay packet (I discovered they were alcoholics, hence the empty pay packet); Sarah, a manic depressive, a condition of which I had never heard, whose wildly fluctuating mood swings made her a frightening person to work with; Andrew, a rugged, handsome playboy who changed his girlfriend every week and could often be seen leaving the fire exit to avoid some irate husband waiting outside the hotel; Gemma, an out of control teenager whose wild exploits kept everyone amused; last but not least, Viv. Viv was a nymphomaniac. Separated from a violent husband, she had experienced a great deal of pain and exploitation in her short life. Of them all, Viv was the kindest to a relatively sheltered fifteen-year-old who had seen little of the real world. She simultaneously 'mothered' and treated me as an equal. Like her, I was mad about motorbikes, and bought a weekly copy of *Motor Cycle News*. Viv paid for me to enter a spot the ball competition to win a Norton Commando 850; sadly someone else spotted the ball first and I had to make do with my much more modest Suzuki 125.

My rootless upbringing made me feel at home with others who were rootless. There was an instinctive bond with these colourful, exciting, life-affirming people. I experienced an affinity with the circumstances of their lives, in their sadnesses and celebrations. Their values, attitudes and lifestyle made them so different from the people I knew through church yet somehow they felt much more like the people Jesus met in the Gospels. For me, if Christian faith was to have any relevance, it must be able to engage and meet these people, my lonely, damaged friends, whose ideas and experiences of relationships made the possibility of a relationship with God an alien concept. The gospel, if it is to be the gospel, has to shake off the safety, respectability, and life-denying scaffolding that so often surrounds it. At this stage I didn't realise that God was going to ask me to go into the Church to help it become the risky, life-affirming, unencumbered place it was always meant to be; in car-speak, to be less the safety-conscious, rubber-bumpered, airbag-laden Volvo and more the soul stirring, aural stimulating, seductively sculptured Ferrari.

My 'call' to be a minister was conventional enough, if somewhat premature, since I had been a Christian for only a year or so. At a missionary meeting held one Sunday, the speaker had powerfully challenged young people to think about serving God. The scope for psychological manipulation in such meetings can be immense but it had no apparent effect on me. Yet several weeks later, the speaker's wife asked me in casual conversation what I was planning to do with my life. Instead of replying with my stock answer 'Go to university', I surprised both her and myself by saying, 'I am going to stand at the front of the church and speak just like the minister'. Where this thought came from I do not know. This instinctive answer must have been a brief manifestation of my unconscious desires. My unconscious did a remarkably good job, in that I promptly and totally forgot this incident until the day of my graduation from theological college eight years later. I met again the wife of the missionary (who had by now become a Baptist minister) who recalled it. At that moment it came flooding back but until then the event had been working away in various unconscious ways.

Falling in love may have had some influence in the repression of these celestial and clerical thoughts. Certainly my conscious thoughts and feelings were consumed by this dramatic new turn of events. There was one member of staff at the Seaview Hotel whom I have not so far mentioned – a normal, quiet, pony-tailed, nineteen-year-old chef called Liz. She rarely ventured out of the kitchen but when I first saw her, my heart went into a paroxysm of activity. She turned, looked at me with her swimming-pool blue eyes and smiled. My emotions dived straight in. I blushed from hair-tip to toenails and became both immobilised and speechless. I surreptitiously found out as much about her as I could without the others guessing. Sadly, I discovered she was going out with someone else and had been for several years. My soaring hopes were shot down in flames. However, all was not lost. One fact of life which I had learned from my fellow waiting staff was that relationships are seldom permanent. When I confided in Viv, she encouraged me to take the risk of asking Liz out. It took me two weeks before I asked her as the anticipated pain of rejection was almost unbearable. When I finally did ask her to go for a drink with me, she looked very surprised before replying 'I'm not sure'. The walls of my world caved in for at least three days. I carried on waiting in the dining room and avoiding the kitchen as much as I could. My spurned emotions turned in another direction. A new girl had arrived at YP that week, a cousin of a church family, visiting Weston-super-Mare for a holiday. Having survived this major risk-taking episode, I thought I had nothing to lose, so I asked Sarah out. We arranged to meet at the bus station on Saturday after work. As I left the hotel, who should be waiting for me but Liz who said, 'Shall we go for that drink then?' It was a Cheddar Gorge sized dilemma. Could I risk saying 'no' to this creature of my adolescent fantasy and dreams? Could I cope with the consequences in the YP group of standing Sarah up? I decided with my heart (or was it my hormones?) rather than my head and said 'Yes'. Liz told me that she had decided to end her relationship with her boyfriend before going out with me, which is why it had taken her some time to say 'yes' to me. We were from very different backgrounds, a middle-class adolescent, old for my age in some ways and naive in others and intent on going to university, and a working-class woman, young for her age and with no particular desire to go anywhere. Unfortunately Sarah waited two hours at the bus station. I was not the most popular person in the YP, but I didn't care. I was in love in all its adolescent intensity. What is special about first love? It is the discovery of uncharted depths and unexpected emotions which one can share with another. For an opposite sex twin it is, I suggest, something more. The fact of being a twin and the influence this has in other relationships, is still for me a shadowy area, but one that surfaces from time to time in my own story. For me it was about an emotional separation from the one who has always been there. Significantly she shared the same Christian name as my twin. Perhaps that was enough to provide security in this new venture. What was exciting was the discovery that someone else wants you as much as you want them.

The nine months of the relationship flew by before finishing abruptly and painfully. As Tom Cruise says in his aviator talk in the film *Top Gun*, I 'crashed and burned'. Liz had moved to work at another hotel and I had moved to the sixth form. I had arranged to collect her on the Sunday afternoon but when I arrived she said that she had promised to iron a shirt for Daniel, one of the waiters. The enormity of my reaction still surprises me today. I felt utterly betrayed, consumed by overwhelming anger and a crushing experience of rejection. I stormed out, saying that she had obviously made her decision, him instead of me. The tears streamed down my face as I rode my motorbike round the head-land to try to escape from the pain, which hung on grimly like some unwelcome pillion passenger.

Painfully, the next few weeks raced by, each day marginally more comfortable than the one before. Life has a way of carrying on. In the course of time I studied for my 'A' levels (English,

Economics and History), acquired another girlfriend (six foot Sue), and bought another motorbike, a 1953 Royal Enfield 250 replica of the Continental GT (and sold it as it proved so unreliable and leaked a pint of oil from the gearbox every week). As I write this I am aware that I am neatly glossing over the pain of rejection and humiliation I felt. There was a poignant and powerful longing in me to see Liz again. I used to dream of some chance encounter and some dramatic reconciliation. Yet there was still a throbbing open emotional wound that shrank in protest when I took any steps to do so. In two years I saw her only once as I was driving past a bus-stop. Even the six-pot caliper disc brakes found on modern superbikes could not have stopped me that day as I kept the motor running and roared off into the distance. My emotions remained in jangled Hydra-like confusion.

This was also the time I rebelled against my father by leaving the Boys' Brigade. It was something he didn't want me to do, so I left in the hope of getting him to take notice of me which he did, especially when I started applying for universities. It felt as if a candle had been lit, bringing a fragile warmth and light into a dark room. He began to talk to me on an adult to adult basis, helped no doubt by his having started an Open University degree. I decided to go to Liverpool University to do a Social Studies degree, a goal whose achievement was to prove much more eventful than I had planned.

In the starlit hours of an early summer morning, the wind whipped across my face as my motorbike accelerated faster and faster and the exhilaration of speed sent the adrenaline coursing round my body. Then it all went horribly wrong. For reasons I still do not know my motorbike left the road and ploughed across a grass verge. My right hand yanked on the front brake lever with no discernible effect, as every muscle strained to keep the motorbike upright. My mind, which recorded the event in slow motion, tells me I was winning the battle, until, that is, I hit a broad area of gravel. The motorbike cartwheeled, throwing me through the air with an uncanny sensation of flying, to land on the ground. Soft skin shredded. Hard bone made contact with harder stone and the warm blackness enveloped me as I lapsed into unconsciousness.

When I came round my body was racked with pain and my head pounded as if some ever-present being was hitting me repeatedly with a sledgehammer. In shock, my first thought was, 'Oh dear, my motorbike won't work' (in fact the front wheel had folded in half and I had to sell the entire machine for scrap). My second and third thoughts were, 'Why is there so much blood?' and 'Why won't my leg work properly?' Undeterred, I started to walk home (in the wrong direction as it turned out), hoping to hitch a lift though it was 2 o'clock in the morning. I must have looked like a character from *Nightmare on Elm Street*, yet some brave soul stopped to give me a lift to the nearest hospital. All I can remember was sitting in the front passenger seat, with my hands cupped together to catch the blood dripping from my face, and apologising profusely for spoiling his car. Whatever pain I had experienced so far was to pale into insignificance when the hospital staff went to work. I remember one nurse saying, 'This may hurt a little' – English understatement at its very best – whilst another nurse held me down and the gravel was scrubbed from my knee.

This accident came at a most unfortunate time, for I was due to sit all my 'A' level exams the following week. Since retakes in English were not possible unless one retook the whole year, I had to take them despite concussion, a leg that wouldn't bend and a face that would have made Frankenstein's monster look handsome. My soul remained in considerably better shape than my body. My young faith could appreciate that the church were praying for me, and at times this became a tangible experience of a God who was at work in my situation, not some remote being to be blamed in an expression of anger. Even in the physically draining three-hour examinations there was a sense of being held – in a metaphysical sense – that somehow made theological and psychological connections.

I did have questions, 'Would my face be badly scarred?', 'Would I still be able to go to university?', 'Would I get another motorbike?', yet there was an underlying peace pervading the experience. Time has answered these questions: my face and knee have small scars; I did pass my exams; I did go to university; and twenty years later I am still riding motorbikes. Life has, however, been anything but peaceful. It has been intriguing to discover, with

23

sensations of *déjà vu*, that the kaleidoscope of feelings, emotions, memories and reflections generated by that motorcycle accident have surfaced again and again, like some gigantic blue whale coming up for oxygen in order to exist and to continue existing.

Life has variously meant fighting for survival, all-encompassing pain, shock and disorientation, a dependence on others (sometimes out of need, sometimes out of choice), prayer, faith, questioning and peace. This 'kaleidoscopic dynamic' has been not only my own, but also one which I have shared repeatedly with those whom I have sought to pastor and counsel, to whom I have listened, for whom I have wept and whose pain I have shared. I have endeavoured to love in fulfilment of Christ's command (Luke 10:27), to share the burdens of others as encouraged by Paul (Gal. 6:2), to be practical in my outworking of faith (Jas 2:17), to model both compassion (I Pet. 3:8) and belonging (I John 3:1–2), thankful for knowledge and experience of an immanent and transcendent God. The paradox of God being near and far is one that I explore further in chapter 10.

Through my own experiences, and those I have shared with others, I am encouraged by Simon Peter's attempt to walk on water (Matt. 14:28–33). Despite all his faults, he did manage several steps before he began to sink; then he was held by Christ. I am more sure than ever that I have been held by Christ and that part of the purpose of my life is to encourage others to take the risk of leaving the boat, despite the ridicule and jibes of the remaining passengers, and to help them discover Christ, both in their triumph, and more commonly, in their failure. The risk of failure, and the fear of being destroyed by it or by parental expectations, is another commonly occurring theme in my pastoral and therapeutic work.

Yet in stark contrast to my efforts, as I encounter Christians, churches and other ministers within my evangelical tradition, I am increasingly concerned that they give the impression that Christianity is a faith without risk. They want the miraculous without the risk of failure and as an avoidance of pain. They want the glory of the resurrection and ascension without the blood, sweat and tears of a crucifixion as the culmination of thirty or so years of incarnate living.[8] In doing so Gerard Hughes suggests they ignore the treasure of the kingdom of God (Matt. 13:44).

> The treasure lies in what you may consider a most unlikely field yourself. It takes most of us a long time and we have many obstacles to overcome before we begin to recognize the field where our treasure is hidden, that is, before we learn to find and accept ourselves, where God is. Until we find ourselves, God remains remote, a shadowy figure.[9]

How I became aware of the treasure of the kingdom in the field of my life, I shall return to in later chapters.

3

❦

YOU'LL NEVER WALK ALONE

The Ordnance Survey map showed a series of closely etched brown lines leading to a marshy plateau. As we struggled up the hillside, we discovered that it was more demanding than we had expected and so it was with a great sense of relief that we reached even ground. The team leader took another quick bearing with map and compass and off we went. In his haste he had slightly miscalculated the direction and the ground became marshier than we had anticipated. We saw no option and continued but before we had gone many paces further a sudden deep bass voice boomed out, 'Don't move another inch'. Another walker was shouting at us from some distance and told us to retrace our tracks. When we met up with him he explained that we were just about to walk into one of the most dangerous bogs on Dartmoor, where he had nearly lost his son. The particular danger was that this bog was very close to a regular path used by hill walkers. The message was clear: a slight, seemingly insignificant miscalculation can have disaster as a consequence. There are times in life when one can look back and see small incidents which had profound consequences.

After finishing my degree at Liverpool, I was asked back to take part in an evangelistic mission organised by the Christian Union. Unwittingly the room allocated to me was my original room at university, E2008 Morton House. As I walked through the entrance door to the block, I was assailed by the distinctive smell of floor polish, stale beer and sweaty feet. I suddenly became anxious, later experiencing overpowering feelings of loneliness. The feelings and emotions of three years earlier, buried deep within my unconscious (as I had been unaware of them at the time) were resurrected by a unique smell. As a 'fresher' I was so busy trying to survive that such feelings were pushed away along with others. Unfortunately I had been assigned to a room on a floor primarily occupied by students who had all decided to stay together for a second year. This meant there was little chance of new students becoming part of the group, whose identity was already established. Either you fitted in, or you didn't. I felt cheated with a depressing sense of *déjà vu* – yet again, if I wanted to be accepted, I had to fit in with a crowd who were not 'my sort of people'.

At least, I thought, I would be welcomed at the Christian Union, which people in my church had encouraged me to join. At the first meeting I heard Roger Forster (later to become famous for the development of the Ichthus Christian Fellowship, a multi-congregation church in South London) speak eloquently about the intellectual credibility of the Christian faith – an important message for me to hear. But that was it. When the meeting ended no one spoke to me and I went home alone. This experience coupled with the juvenile antics of several Christians in Morton House (the slang terms 'nerds' or 'anoraks' had not yet been invented) turned me off the CU. I still regularly attended church – trying out Roman Catholic, Anglican, House Church, Baptist, Brethren and Strict Baptist denominations; read the Bible; prayed; and talked about my faith. My faith deepened because as people questioned me, encouraged by Roger Forster's example, I came to accept Christian belief as a credible, intellectual faith for myself, not merely because I had been brought up in it or taught it at church. I later came to understand this in terms of James Fowler's stages of faith development.[1] Drawing on the work of Erikson, Piaget and Kohlberg and on interviews with over five hundred people, Fowler developed a seven-stage developmental model related to human growth and development through the life cycle.

Stage 0 is primal faith, where faith is a simple pre-linguistic trust by an infant in their care-giver. Stage 1 is intuitive-projective faith, forming between the ages of two and six, where a child constructs meaning by using imagination and the powerful images it contains. These images are used to interpret experience but no

27

concepts are yet available to order these intellectually. Stage 2 is mythic-literal faith. The child from six to eleven begins to think literally about the world. Story-telling is crucial to development but abstract thinking is not yet a major feature. 'Though this stage has its rise typically in middle childhood, researchers find many adolescents and a fair number of adults best described by this stage.'[2] Stage 3 is synthetic-conventional faith. The adolescent has now the ability to think abstractly, which develops a whole new dimension of belief possibilities but it is also a stage which raises questions of conformity. 'Many adults of all ages seem to have equilibrated their growth in identity and faith at this stage, and continue to be particularly dependent upon interpersonal relations and the external authority of groups or institutional roles for maintaining the shape of their identity or faith.'[3] Stage 4 is individuative-reflective faith, when people in their late teens and twenties begin to develop critical beliefs and values that are not so dependent upon others. There emerges 'a capacity for dialogue between the selves others see and a self "accessible only to me"'[4] and a 'critical distancing from one's previous value system'.[5] Stage 5 is conjunctive faith, where a re-evaluation of faith meaning created in previous stages results in a critical openness and an awareness of polarities and ambiguities. Stage 6 is universalising faith, which few attain to and which focuses on the self finding a 'true depth through a grounding in Being'.[6] Fowler cites Martin Luther King and Bonhoeffer as examples.[7]

Fowler sees people being able to keep on growing in faith terms, at whatever stage of the developmental process they find themselves. Each decade of life, with the fresh challenges it brings allows the hope of new beliefs and values which flow out of the psychological growth of the person. Conversely it also explains why some people find their lives out of harmony with their beliefs and values, that may have become static or rooted in an earlier stage of faith development. I had passed from a synthetic-conventional faith stage which consisted of 'a personal and largely unreflective synthesis of beliefs and values [used] to support identity and to unite one in emotional solidarity with others'[8] to the start of an individuative-reflective faith stage which consisted of 'critical reflection on one's beliefs and values, understanding of the self. . .and the assumption of responsibility for making choices of ideology.'[9] Part of this process was reflected in trying to be part of the CU, not as a refuge from loneliness, (though it was this too) but because it was a group who shared my own beliefs, such as they were at this stage. Was this any worse than the usual eighteen year old leaving home? My answer now is 'yes' and 'no'. My twin sister had married a month before I went away to Liverpool, the significance of which was that this was the first time I was truly alone. Home was now different as Elizabeth was now part of someone else. I needed to forge a new identity for 'me' that was truly distinct but the unconscious pattern was of a need to be close to others.

While I felt I never had the opportunity to 'fit in' in Hall, I did meet a good crowd of students in the Social Studies Society which, because of the fragmented nature of the course had its own common room at the university. This was where I 'hung out' and joined in our speciality – 'partying'. For the inner loneliness and unconscious patterning, I found an external answer – girl-friends. The relationships were fun, but immature and short-lived like emotional Kleenex paper hankies, used once then discarded. There was something not quite right somewhere in this pattern. I didn't understand then, as I do now, that I was using women in this way because I was angry with them. I was unaware of the depth of my emotional pain until I went home that Easter. I went back to work at the Seaview Hotel but could not have imagined what would happen. As I walked into the dining room I was introduced to the new head waiter, Daniel; the same Daniel whom I had last seen with Liz. Daniel the rival, competitor and victor. Daniel whom I loathed with a staggering emotion. Politeness ruled as I shook his hand, our eyes locked in hostile gaze before he looked away. I heard a familiar laugh and looking over his shoulder, I saw Liz. For the second time I was jabbed by an emotional blow that felt way below the belt. She froze, her eyes widened, blushed a delicate shade of pink, smiled and walked on by. She was working temporarily as a waitress. A surge of turbulent feelings overwhelmed me – love, affection, anger, happiness and sadness. Later that day she met me on my own like some clan-destine rendezvous and told me that they were getting engaged that evening. That afternoon I waited for her on the same bench where she had once waited for me, knowing that Daniel had to work late and I asked her to go for a drink. Liz communicated surprise and happiness, becoming shy like a young adolescent girl. We drove to Sand Bay where we sat and talked. I said whatever came into my head and heard myself, much to my surprise, talking of my feelings of pain and rejection over the way our relationship had ended. It was an emotional baring of my soul, fraught with risk, yet one I found to be infinitely releasing. Liz explained her confusion and her own feelings of rejection. It was, I recall, a warm balmy evening, as we sat outside watching the sky display red and orange shades of warmth and colour. I learnt about the pain I caused her. How my rejection by her, more alert to the fact that the relationship had run its course and that the social and cultural differences were increasing, had resulted in my rejection of her. As we embraced it seemed that time stood still when in the words of a Joe Cocker song, we 'let the healing begin'. This experience gave me insight into the power of relationships, the unconscious factors underlying them, the damage caused by incomplete endings and the healing that can come from letting a relationship go. I drove Liz to her home to the obvious consternation of her soon to be fiancé and her parents, leaving her to explain whatever she wanted.

Why had this relationship been so significant? Why had I walked out on her originally? Did I feel threatened by Daniel, thus exposing a deep layer of insecurity in me? Had she really wanted me or was I the reason to escape from a previous relationship she felt trapped in? Was there an element of an earlier betrayal, either real or perceived? Was I in competition with my twin who was successfully entering into a relationship at the same time? The questions multiply as they do whenever we really sit down and explore what is going on beneath the surface of our lives. What I do know is that the subterranean anger that once flowed powerfully and influenced so many relationships had overnight dwindled to a stream. Henri Nouwen talks about the wounded healer (a theme we will return to in chapter 10); it is no surprise to me that so many of the people I see as a pastoral counsellor are seeking someone who can listen to their anger and pain at severed relationships. They don't know me but it is almost as if their unconscious senses someone who knows and feels what is so important to them. I cannot of course feel their exact pain and do not claim to do so. It is more that I am alert to the underlying feelings. I possess an openness to their feelings that allows me to hear their individual story. Truly here one can see the Spirit of God at work in a way that is rarely acknowledged yet is a vital element on the journey to wholeness.

Going back to university had a very different feel to it that summer term. My psychological growth had in fact given me a fresh confidence and security in who I was and this in turn led to a new phase of spiritual growth and activity. I made contact with the CU again, becoming the CU rep. for the Social and Environmental Studies faculty. I also agreed to go on an evangelistic mission run by the CU at a new church in Runcorn after the exams. This time I was warmly welcomed, not knowing it was to lead to a dramatic theological encounter. The daily Bible studies focused on the Holy Spirit as a genuine member of the Trinity, the 'oneness' and the 'threeness' of God. During the afternoons we undertook door-to-door visitation on a tough concrete-jungle housing estate where I saw answers to prayer, and more importantly, answers to my prayers. This communicated to me that God wanted me as a part of his kingdom. It was as though the Spirit of God had somehow shepherded me back into the fold. While I never felt I was like the prodigal son in Luke 15, I did experience a homecoming and a welcome back into the family. I also met a couple of larger than life characters, Dave and Paul. They had become Christians in their first week at university and their enthusiasm was both infectious and completely 'over the top'. This gave them a charisma and status, so when I was asked to share a house with them in the next academic year, I really felt I had arrived. I became just like them because I wanted to be noticed and, in doing so, discovered the subtle allure of power and control over others. No matter what others did, we did it in a bigger and better way. If someone prayed for an hour, we could do it for two. While there was a genuine Christian love and commitment expressed by this, at this stage none of us had the maturity to realise quite what else was going on. Insofar as this psychological need to belong was allied to what I would now describe as a false, shallow or super spirituality, we were able to influence others in a way that I find quite frightening. There is a dynamic which manipulates people to conform to certain unspoken rules, which in Christian Unions are about the content and subculture of evangelicalism.[10] Nowadays I have huge questions about the subculture associated with evangelicalism as well as its inability to be self-critical or self-aware.[11] One of the dangers in possessing the truth is that we no longer question it, we simply appeal to it. As these groups consist of young students they are unlikely to be able to separate social pressure from biblical belief. When I was a student, drinking alcohol was frowned upon and one of the things that 'proper' and 'committed' members of the CU did not do. I, of course, took not the slightest notice of this but the pressure to conform was still experienced. Nowadays if I spoke at a CU and suggested that drinking wasn't a proper Christian thing to do, they would be mystified, as attitudes in our culture have changed and all I would be doing was imposing the viewpoint of my subculture but using the Bible to authenticate a subcultural point of view as 'truth'. In the work I have done with students ever since, I have attempted to model an intellectual rigour with a down-to-earth spirituality that is not afraid of questions about meaning, without feeling I have to have all the answers or need to defend God.

My growing interest in the Holy Spirit was inadequate preparation for the impact of Charismatic renewal when it hit the CU like a tidal wave, with just as devastating consequences. Before I arrived the CU had been split down the middle, like some neatly cleaved joint of meat. The Bible became a weapon to be used like some bloody axe in hand-to-hand combat. When along with, and led by Dave and Paul, I became a leader in the CU, the issue of who the Spirit was and what he did was now on my agenda. Each of us responded in different ways. Dave's agenda concerned the fear of God and the joy of Christ. Paul's was an enthusiasm for an experience of baptism in the Spirit and mine was a commitment to aggressive evangelism. My Christocentric faith, primarily but not completely intellectual, was to be transformed into an experiential encounter where Jesus brought salvation and the Spirit brought power. Power, especially spiritual power, is addictive because it can be concealed so cunningly and under such a saintly guise. This is an issue I will explore further in chapter 8.

Before this mission encounter with Dave and Paul something else took place. Another student doing Social Studies, who lived in Liverpool, after registering some surprise that I was a Christian (the feeling was mutual) invited me to her church youth group. Group Four, as it was known, met in the outhouse of an old farmhouse in Maghull (an outer northern suburb of Liverpool) and was part of a Brethren Assembly. This group of young people showed to me that it was possible to both enjoy God and have a good time. This highlighted to me the dualistic life I was leading, 'partying' with my friends in Social Studies and praying with my friends in the CU. With Group Four I could do both. I was struck by their kindness as well, because on my nineteenth birthday, knowing that I was in the middle of exams, one of them (Judy) had organised them all to send me birthday cards. I was very touched although it was only later I discovered her ulterior motives. The summer intervened and I went home. Yet it was that summer as part of another evangelistic mission that I read these life-changing words in Matthew 9:35–8,

> Jesus went through all the towns and villages, teaching in their synagogues, preaching the good news of the kingdom and healing every disease and sickness. When he saw the crowds, he had compassion on them, because they were harassed and helpless, like sheep without a shepherd. Then he said to the disciples, 'The harvest is plentiful but the workers are few. Ask the Lord of the harvest, therefore, to send out workers into the harvest field.'

This was another metaphysical encounter where space and time stood still and combined with an overwhelming sense of God's presence to produce in me a knowing in an instant that this call was for me. One paraphrase of this passage puts it this way: 'Jesus . . .healed their bruised and hurt lives. When he looked out over the crowds, his heart broke.' My own experience and those broken and bruised people I worked with and encountered as I

visited homes in needy areas drew from me a response of compassion and a prayer, 'Lord, if you want me to be one of those
workers, here I am.' This was much more genuinely me than the
emphasis I was to place on the Spirit and aggressive evangelism
when back with the CU. Groups are able to influence powerfully
the way individuals act and react as we shall explore later in
chapter 8.

An unexpected consequence of living in a house with Dave,
Paul and others arose out of the fact that the landlord was the
vicar of the local Anglican church. One reason for our low rent
was the expectation that we would help out at St Cleopas, in the
Dingle, part of Toxteth, a troubled inner-city ghetto. On Fridays
we ran a club for 12–14 year olds who normally hung round the
street corners. We attempted to organise games, play music and
do a God-spot – which meant preaching at them. They attempted
to sabotage everything and usually succeeded as a group of university students were no match for a bunch of teenage streetwise
scousers. I can still remember the curate, John Whitley, trying to
suggest that an incarnational approach might be more successful.
We of course, Spirit-filled and Bible-believing, knew better. None
of us knew what an incarnational approach was, and we never
bothered to find out. The Friday evenings came to an end when
one of the ring-leaders ended up in a remand centre at Risley,
known as 'Grisley Risley'. He robbed a man who was with a
prostitute in a car on Otterspool Promenade, a local 'tarts' venue,
leaving the man with a gash in his face requiring twenty stitches.

This had, nevertheless, been a very educative experience; we
had been drawn into the reality of life in the inner area of a then
declining city with unemployment levels running at 25 per cent
for whites and 45 per cent for blacks. I was not then aware of the
term 'underclass' but painfully aware of the despair that stalks such
urban priority areas like a blood-sucking vampire. We had been
working with the 'good' kids who would regularly attack the
police and overturn patrol cars for fun. In turn they would be
beaten up by the police and 'fitted up' for burglaries, vandalism
and the like that they had not done. According to their 'law of
the concrete jungle' this was fair, as there were many other 'crimes'
they had committed that they had not been 'done' for. It was out

of this tinderbox environment that the Toxteth riots took place in 1981. A key figure in mediating during this period of lawlessness was the Revd Colin Bedford (our landlord) who demonstrated along with his family the real meaning of incarnation, described in his book *Weep for the City*.

The theological lesson I learnt from this was that preaching at people, as opposed to *for* people is of little value. And it is just as easy for the Church to retreat into its buildings and convince itself that it has done its job. That would be like the captain of the *Titanic* suggesting his dinner guests wear something warm as forecasts suggested that it might be a bit chilly. Living out the gospel, patiently, slowly, with many setbacks, building relationships, establishing hope, demonstrating love and acceptance, refusing to be bullied by any authority and forced into accommodation speaks of incarnation before proclamation. Job's friends who sat with him in the midst of his turmoil and pain 'blew it' as soon as they opened their mouths.[12] There is a right time and a right place for proclamation but it is too easy to see that as the short cut that avoids the trauma of others' broken lives. We so focus on the last three years of Jesus' life that we forget the first thirty.[13]

Life at university was an enjoyable, hectic turmoil of work, playing basketball, doing evangelism in the students' union, going to parties at the Liver Buildings and seeing Judy. It didn't take me too long to realise that this was the woman for me but it raised the issue of commitment. I was learning about risking and trusting in my relationship with Judy. The urgent need just to have a girlfriend as an antidote to aloneness was gone but I now faced a major decision. Marriage for life is a long commitment and one that both excited me and frightened me. I loved her gentleness, her care, her smile, her laugh, her sense of fun and big blue eyes, but I was not always sure. Judy's perception is that I gave her a rough time, of being unsure whether I was serious or not, dropping her for someone else, coming back a week later saying I still wanted to be a 'good friend', and going out with her again. It felt to me to be a risk which, impelled by love, I wanted to take. Judy's risk was very different. A family-loving, suburban Liverpudlian from a Brethren background, she had no desire to

leave Liverpool, her church or her family. At times I felt like a
burglar trying to break into the Tower of London to snatch away
the crown jewels. Yet it was a risk we both agreed to take, borne
along by our relationship with each other and our relationship
with God.

Risk is at the heart of any real relationship. At this stage I did
not feel secure enough as a person or know myself well enough
to reveal to others what I was really like. I liked the paradoxical
attention of being a 'rebel' yet also a committed Christian who
was a leader in the CU. This had an additional element of respect
because I was also going to be a minister. Following my 'call' I
had worked with my church in Weston-super-Mare for a summer
as an assistant to the minister. This had confirmed the direction I
wanted to pursue and this had been recognised by the church, the
regional Baptist Association and the theological college I had
applied to train at.

Where was that vulnerable, lonely part of me, terrified at being
on the outside? That Alistair was kept well hidden. In effect I
colluded with the norms of the evangelicalism of the Christian
Union and appeared as a confident, colourful leader of others,
addicted to the pursuit of power and attention and like all genuine
addicts denying that this was the case. I read all the right books,
the then current favourite being J.I. Packer's *Knowing God*. I
attended all the prayer meetings, read the Bible each day and
witnessed to anyone, anywhere. On one occasion I was travelling
on a train and just happened to have 200 tracts in my pocket, so
after a quick prayer, went up and down the carriages giving these
evangelistic leaflets out. This evangelical emphasis, nurtured by
meeting such speakers as Nick Cuthbert (the leader of a multi-
congregation church in Birmingham), led to dramatic but one-
sided growth as a Christian. I was actually playing safe and avoiding
taking risks. I think it is significant that I have no friends left from
this time. Dave, Paul and others with whom I spent so much time,
were always rivals or competitors but never friends. What has been
good, however, arising out of the writing of this book, is meeting
up with Dave again almost twenty years later. We are living in the
same city, both working for the Church, and have rediscovered
this time in our past and are exploring a friendship for the future.

Theologically we have both changed and matured in unexpected but exciting ways.

Hindsight is a dangerous thing in its ability to manufacture regrets. I have regrets about this time as a student. I wish I had spent more time simply being a student, playing football for the Social Studies team, going with the Anglican chaplaincy to Iona, spending weekends parachuting, exploring other forms of spirituality, with more time given to self-awareness rather than to frenetic, 'look aren't I a good boy, God?' activity. Yet it was several years later and from the relative security provided by marriage to Judy, that I was able to move into these uncharted waters and begin to explore the fathomable depths looking for buried treasure. Getting married was the next task on my agenda.

4

❧

THE GOOD, THE BAD AND THE UGLY

The next five years are best described by the title of one of Clint Eastwood's spaghetti Westerns. Yet it is too simplistic to 'split' it into separate sections, like 'goodies' and 'baddies' in a children's game. As one film critic said, 'it is difficult to tell them apart and they all looked ugly'. Reflecting now, I realise there were some very positive and some very negative experiences during this time but they were often enmeshed in one another and grew out of each other.

I spent the year between finishing university and getting married living at home with my parents in Weston-super-Mare, which I found somewhat of a trial, having become used to my freedom. It seems that mothers never want their sons to grow up or leave them for another and I was eager to leave and be free of the manipulative family dynamics.[1] I was working for British Rail in Bristol which at least gave me the option of free or reduced-rate travel to Liverpool to see Judy every three weeks or so. Working with a group of working-class men, intent on educating me about the 'real' world before I went off to be a 'vicar', was eventful to say the least. I was pitched headlong into a world of gnawing bitterness, petty jealousies, half-truths and lies, the sleaze of pornography, the incompetence and lack of concern by managers, a world peopled by characters living in fantasies of their own making, that bore little relation to reality. Some were further stressed by addictions to sex, alcohol and gambling. If ever any people needed good news it was this group of men. It made me realise how much harder it was both to be genuinely Christian

38

and to talk to men. Over the year I had the opportunity to talk to each of the men about what I believed and why, though only once or twice at most. They would ask questions when they thought others were not listening. Others unburdened their lives like a penitent confessing to a priest. Evangelism here was more about listening and entering into the pain of others, than telling them they needed to be saved. What I was able to do, having heard them, was to give them choices, including the choice of faith or not.

It was during this period that I went back to university for a week to take part in a mission. Something of great significance took place that week, as I found myself spending more time listening to Christians sharing their problems than I did talking to people about Christianity. This in itself was surprising given the reputation that I had had in the CU of being involved in upfront, no-holds-barred proclamation. I had changed, in that the experiences at work had widened my somewhat blinkered vision and I was now being much more the person who was actually 'me', rather than living up to some stereotype. As I talked about this with the colleague I was working with she recommended I read a book called *Winter Past. A story of depression and healing* by Nancy Smith. I read it avidly and in doing so discovered a whole new universe. Nancy had to leave a mission team because of paralysis in both legs, caused not by any physiological problem but by an hysterical reaction. As a result she became depressed and felt she had completely failed God. She went to see a psychotherapist who helped her uncover an experience of sexual abuse, which had caused her psychological trauma. I remember being deeply moved by this story and at the end I put the book down and prayed, 'Lord, I want to heal people like that psychotherapist'. At this stage I did not even know what a psychotherapist was, as the term had not been explained in the book. If I had known what was going to be involved, I might not have been so impetuous, yet it was a prayer of faith that God answered in his own surprising way. The evangelistic mission finished and I went home to prepare for my wedding later in the summer. Yet a new mission had begun in me. My missionary journey was not to be to the ends of the earth and its dark subcontinents, but to the inner world and its dark subconscious, bringing the shalom, the wholeness of God. Yet I was an all-too-fragile messenger.

As the radiant bride in shimmering white walked down the aisle, I felt the happiest person alive. Slowly, graciously, Judy moved along the centre of the church, her quivering lip the only indicator of the excitement and nervousness of the occasion. The hymns, prayers, vows and sermon all passed in a speeding blur. The preacher spoke about Abraham and Sarah as they embarked on an adventurous and, at times, uncomfortable journey of life and faith. They were to prove prophetic words. Following the reception and a car chase around the centre of Liverpool by friends wanting to discover our honeymoon destination, we arrived at our hotel and on the Monday we were to fly to Corfu.

After an exhausting day we slept as best we could in view of the unfamiliarity of discovering someone else in what each of us thought was our own bed. The next day dawned revealing a bleak sky dominated by grey, rain-rich clouds. After breakfast it poured with torrential rain outside and Judy cried torrential tears inside. Feelings of loss and abandonment were never far from the surface, mingled with a genuine joy at being married. I was to discover that for Judy the loss of parents, sisters, friends, job and home was a desolating experience. It is a testimony to her love for me that she was willing to risk such major changes. We went for a walk to find somewhere for our evening meal – but there is something depressing about a town centre where every shop is closed, the rain descending, the sky leaden and the wind bitingly cold. Monday came, and what a difference a day makes! The sun shone and we were on our way to Corfu – but not before the customs officials had a laugh at the amount of confetti that exuded from every piece of hand luggage. The honeymoon was not exactly disastrous but neither was it full of romantic bliss and contentment. Our room in the hotel was above the kitchens where work started at 5 a.m., and next to the bar which closed at 2 a.m. After numerous complaints we were given other rooms, although Judy was sick in the middle of the night and much to her disgust I slept soundly through the entire event. The days were spent on the beach, where I read Wenham's *Elements of New Testament Greek* in preparation for an examination I had to sit when starting at a Baptist Theological College, two weeks after our honeymoon.

What is a theological college like? Stained glass images of earnest, devoted, prayerful, godly men (women then sadly accounted for only 5 per cent of students) were soon shattered. As new students we were allocated a study area called 'the cloisters' and after an Old Testament lecture, Mike (one of our year group) was discussing the idea that several source documents were used in the production of the book of Genesis. As he had come from a fundamentalist church background, Mike denounced such ideas, emphasising his point by frequent thumping of a large black Bible (authorised version). Two other students were arguing with Mike saying that the Bible was not at all reliable and any insights that scholarship could give us should be accepted without question. This infuriated Mike, by now red in the face with moustache bristling, who questioned why they were at theological college at all. They were, of course, 'winding him up' which people always think is fun until they in turn are wound up. Yet the word 'wound' has two meanings as well as two pronunciations – it is either the past tense of wind, or damage inflicted to the body, feelings or reputation. Some would say that this incident was 'just a laugh' or 'character forming'. Was it so awful that I laughed along with everyone else? With hindsight, I see it as a pattern for our year group, a pattern which in some way grew out of the ethos of the College and the evangelicalism it represented. In our year there appeared to be a need among the students to dominate, to be in control. There was an aggressive, competitive edge that I had already experienced in the CU. It was something of a shock to be in the college which had been the subject of so much prayer, conversation, and financial and personal sacrifice, only to discover that I and my contemporaries were not the most pleasant or the most caring people.

Over that summer the College had found us a flat, the upper two floors of a Victorian house owned by a Miss Harris, who lived on the ground floor. She was a formidable lady with forthright views, but the flat did provide plenty of space at a very reasonable rent. We moved in our assorted collection of third and fourth-hand furniture and set up our first home in September

1979, two weeks before College started. Judy had found a job as an administrator for a Social Services area office, a few miles away. Transport came in the shape of a metallic blue Honda 400 Superdream motorbike. Friday was shopping day, so I would arrive outside the office, to find Judy waiting with four full carrier bags. She would get on and a friend would then give her the carrier bags which she balanced on her knees as we carefully rode home. If only life was as easy as balancing those carrier bags. Judy was dreadfully homesick and I used to walk to the nearest public phone box and ring her parents twice a week as she could not face hearing their voices without seeing them. Work was no refuge either as it transpired that Judy's boss was a particularly difficult woman who expected Judy to do jobs she was not trained to do and who alienated the people from whom Judy then needed to obtain information.

In effect Judy experienced an extended period of mourning for the loss of her family, her church, her home and her friends. The uprooting was traumatic and one that I did not fully appreciate, since moving had been a way of life for me. I did not help matters as I was absent, sitting in the kitchen upstairs, failing miserably in my struggle to learn both Greek and Hebrew, because I had little comprehension of basic language structure. That first term I spent hours trying to do the work for the next day and thinking very unchristian thoughts about fellow students who could do it in twenty minutes. Most evenings Judy was abandoned to a small black and white portable television in a large, cold lounge. This was hardly the best start to a marriage and so we decided to do something about it. I explored with several people the way ahead and in the end we decided to go for some counselling at the Westminster Pastoral Foundation. When I had prayed that I, like psychotherapists, could help others, I (with the naïveté of youth) had not envisaged that the place to begin with was me. Over a six-month period a great deal happened. Most of all, I learned the value of being listened to. I felt valued and was given time, acceptance, where I could share the burden of my grief, my loneliness, my frustration, my indecision and my guilt. I was able to think my thoughts aloud and, sometimes, find answers, or at least discover where to look for them. This initial introduction to counselling was to prepare for a longer time in therapy at a later stage of my journey.

I also became aware of my own intuitive understanding of people, especially when exploring their pain. This came from an exploration of my own, a pain heightened by the fact that I felt I could not tell anyone what was going on for us, and I was burdened by the idea that I had let God down in some unfathomable way. I am amazed now at the immaturity of this response, yet it is one I have encountered again and again as people from an evangelical background come to me for pastoral counselling. 'Why can't God just deal with it by prayer?' I both asked then and am asked now. 'What is it about my church tradition that fails to help people engage with an accepting, loving God, which of course is the heart of the gospel we so assiduously proclaim?'

What was happening to us also paralleled in some measure what was happening to our closest friends, Mike and Julie. They came from Birkenhead on the opposite side of the Mersey to Liverpool so for all of us there was a natural affinity (as in many respects I had adopted Liverpool as home during my time at university there). Julie felt many of the same feelings as Judy, so it was encouraging to know that others were in the same situation as ourselves.

Julie soon discovered she was pregnant, which created problems for Mike. They had no financial support other than Julie working and when he told the Vice-Principal his news, he was given a very cold reception and asked how could he have been so stupid as to allow himself to get in this position. Later conversations with the Principal did not help either as they reinforced this negative message, that money mattered before people. Sadly Julie had a miscarriage that Christmas and Mike refused, because of the pressure he had experienced, to try to have another child. Julie was bewildered and confused by this and saw it as an unforgivable intrusion by the College into their lives. To heighten matters, her mother died that spring and her sense of loss was overwhelming. She felt marooned and alone (Mike being so taken up with College life) in an alien and hostile environment. They were living in the bottom half of a house occupied by a middle-aged single minister, who, they were shocked to discover, was visited by a series of young boys who sometimes appeared scantily clad around the house. Mike complained to the College but was told there was nothing they could do. Mike's trust in the College was again dashed, as the divorce between theory and practice was highlighted once more. It appeared to be acceptable to believe something without living it out. It all came to a head when Mike suffered a nervous breakdown just before the exams in the summer. Julie was still grief-stricken, unable to express the anger which she had buried, and which was to explode with destructive effect several years later.

These were our friends and it was tragic to see Julie lose, in the course of a year, a child, her mother, her husband, and a great deal of her faith. Something 'died' in Julie's ability to trust God and she came to resent all that the College stood for. The College, with all its principles, failed Mike and Julie. Any help which did come, was too little and too late.

At College, that competitive hothouse of male macho spirituality, I did well. I enjoyed the academic work, and gained a good grounding in theology. It is difficult to imagine then, how little I knew but I do remember writing an essay on the kingdom of God, a subject of which I had never heard. Yet it was the start of a liberating, life-enhancing, God-revealing, person-affirming whirlwind of thoughts and ideas called 'theology'. In a review of a recent book on theology, I described Peter Hodgson's *Winds of the Spirit: A Constructive Christian Theology* as a rollercoaster of a book. One moment there is the excitement of climbing to the theological heights where one's vision of God is enlarged, only to plunge into the depths of philosophical, pluralistic and post-modern thinking where words, images and ideas about God have become barely recognisable as having any distinct theological meaning. My time at College gave me some solid ground to stand on when the ride comes to a halt. It was here that my theology became fully Trinitarian in that I learnt about God as Father, Son and Spirit, the One and the Three; and in my theology tutor saw an encouraging example of someone who lived theology in what seemed an integrated way.

Yet I began to question the modus operandi of the College. As one of the three elected student representatives I attempted to raise the profile of married students. The ethos of the College was geared towards the single, male, living-in student; in other words it had not changed since various members of staff had trained, even though most questioned whether it was really 'good enough' for them even when they trained. The idea of providing a crèche was dismissed as 'uneconomic' and the suggestion that wives be allowed to come to lectures (and share in some way what their husbands were learning) was dismissed as inappropriate. For most practical purposes, other than the weekly wives' group, wives were excluded from College, despite the fact that many, like Mike and myself, were dependent on their wives' income to pay for their time there. This clash of ideas came to a head when I booked a guest speaker to come to our termly evening communion service, one occasion to which wives were invited. I asked him to speak about the family – a suitable topic for Kevin who was the director of a children's home. He recounted to the whole College community what he had shared with us as students in lectures. He talked about the vital importance of the family in society and in the Church and suggested that it should therefore fit into College life. He explored the idea that what we learnt about family life during our training was in fact modelled to us by the lecturers. The Principal was furious and demanded to see me first thing next morning after prayers. I was verbally 'dressed down' for 'setting up' the faculty for inappropriate criticism and involvement. It was not up to me or Kevin to tell them what to do. I was shaken. Shaken by the fact that as a student representative I had talked and prayed with this man every week for two years; that I had shared with him, as a spiritual father figure, some of my innermost struggles – only to have it flung back in my face. How could someone have misunderstood me so completely?

It is always a painful discovery that the people we put on pedestals can be all too human, just like ourselves. It was in many respects a final nail in the coffin. It confirmed for me a dangerous undercurrent in my church tradition that so values clarity when it comes to revelation, propositional truth and knowledge of God; that asks for academic and biblical integrity yet appears to be harsh and unfeeling about the human predicaments of ordinary people. Such a tradition breeds offspring who perpetuate a macho Christianity which negates feelings and emotions. Frank Lake, to whom the theology tutor had introduced me, describes this 'split' as a 'schizoid affliction' in this way:

> We who are academic types . . . By the time we have climbed to the top of this or that intra-psychic tower . . . the dread in the dungeons has been thoroughly dissociated and repressed, existing only in the not-me aspects of the self that come up from time to time in dreams. We may know little of the activities still going on in the dungeons.[2]

Lake saw in himself and others the temptation to remain secure in some intra-psychic ivory tower rather than getting down into the dungeon where the real work needs to be done. Similarly, a danger that the Evangelical Church needs to face is its schizoid approach to life, in which right theology is more important than right practice. The person who calls attention to this or challenges some of these assumptions is likely to be regarded with suspicion: anyone who persists faces an unspoken but very real exile. To be pushed to the boundaries, the fringes of a community, to feel somehow not acceptable for asking important and real questions is in my thinking a Christ-denying action. I was however just discovering what it is like to be a scapegoat. It is ironic that the word was invented by William Tyndale in his translation of the Bible into English, yet here in a theological college committed to making the Bible live, there was the psychological process of scapegoating still at work.[3] The full force of this scapegoating process was to be experienced by another, described in detail in chapter 8.

At one stage I thought, 'Surely I must have got this all wrong'. I appreciated and was part of many positive aspects of College life. It offered a wide range of experiences, tutors who helped me to start to think for myself, the pastoral studies year (year four) gave us a great deal of freedom in which the tutor trusted me with his pastoral group while he was away on a term's sabbatical leave (to the evident disapproval of some staff members). I enjoyed playing rugby and football, even though I had to go to the Principal's garden and ask if we could have our ball back. There were many hilarious moments. One of these was being asked to speak evangelistically at a weekend's coaching session held at the National Sports Centre at Crystal Palace for under-16 county hockey players. I entered the hall unsure of what to expect, only to be confronted by sixty sweaty girls in their hockey kit, having just completed one training session and awaiting the next. I was the 'filling' in the middle of the sandwich, just about to be eaten. It slowly dawned on me that I was the only male in the room. Now I realised what the female students at College felt like. Someone wolf-whistled, laughter erupted and I blushed a deep shade of beetroot red, but then had to proceed with my ten-minute evangelistic talk, after which the girls applauded by banging their hockey sticks on the wooden floor before trooping out for their next game. I won't repeat some of the suggestive comments made by a few as they filed past.

Despite the good things, the nagging feeling that all was not well persisted. At times there was a sense of dislocation similar to that curious sensation of not knowing what is dream and what is reality. If anything this sense became stronger when I attended a hospital chaplains' course at a psychiatric hospital. Going to Claybury was like entering a new world. Until then my knowledge of mental illness had been gained from reading Ken Kesey's book *One Flew Over the Cuckoo's Nest* and watching Jack Nicholson's riveting and Oscar-winning performance in the film of the same name. Instinctive first impressions are often more accurate than we imagine after we have begun the process of rationalisation. Claybury bombarded me with images of neglect, decay, bewilderment, as people shambled along prison-like corridors. The graffiti scratched on a wooden seat said it all – 'This place is scary'. Yet amongst this group of psychologically rootless people, I felt curiously at home. I did not feel scared. Claybury was Britain's leading pioneer in the 1950s of the use of entire wards as therapeutic communities, and the strong emphasis on groups remained. Chaplains had been intimately involved with this development and so on acute admission wards, the chaplains ran group therapy sessions. As a student attached to the chaplains' department for the duration of the course, I spent a month on the same ward, discovering that I had a natural aptitude for group therapy. So much so that the Free Church chaplain asked me to cover his role over the subsequent summer. Thus began an experiential training in group therapy. I also used the time to reflect on myself and the growth that I needed to do 'for me'. I was greatly helped in this by the chaplain, Peter, who in this short time facilitated more acceptance and more understanding of myself than had the previous three years. He saw his role as rubbing off some of the rough edges of this young, rather intense theological student, who challenged the way he operated. Peter did this by sending me to visit some long-term patients suffering from dementia. Such patients gave me no verbal clue to whether they had understood anything I had said in the entire time I was with them. I lapsed into silence and began to experience what it was to 'be' with people. I no longer tried to convert them but assured them of a visit from another human being, willing to reach out and touch, often holding their hand as I held them before God in prayer. I did have opportunities to share my faith but it was with the staff and this only after I had earned the right to speak. During this time some of my feelings became clear in a remarkably vivid dream that I subsequently drew as part of one of our exercises. I drew a picture of the College and out of the door came different members of the faculty dressed as Charles Bronson, the central character in the violent series of *Death Wish* films, dispensing slices of Christmas cake with one hand whilst holding Magnum .45 handguns in the other. The brooding sense of menace chilled the sunlit scene as we waited on the lawn. To challenge the status quo of the College and the evangelicalism that it represented was to my unconscious mind a form of 'death wish', certainly something that was injurious to one's health and reputation, yet it was something I was intimately involved with and a foundational part of my being.

One of the consequences of this time was that in conjunction with Ruth, the wife of another student, I ran a self-awareness group. I had obtained the Principal's permission on the condition that he did not have to attend (he did have a sense of humour!) and (I quote) 'you don't leave me with lots of casualties'. I mentioned this development to my year group who either completely ignored it, were very suspicious as if they would be contaminated in some way or who told me they had far better things to do. A group of ten students from other years did start the group and for some it proved a life-changing encounter. Some discovered more about themselves in the six sessions we ran than in all their time at College. While running this group I also used the free day in my fourth year to help two psychiatric social workers with the running of a psychodrama group at Claybury. Deirdrie and Judith were great fun. Both committed feminists they thought it was intriguing to have a male 'vicar' to work with and our conversations ranged over female sexuality, 'all men are bastards', religion, and psychoanalysis (Deirdrie was undergoing a four-sessions-a-week analysis) and anything in between. At that time I tried writing my first booklet on mental illness (rejected by a publisher and a magazine but subsequently rewritten and published as *Out of the Maze*) and they were very supportive of this project. I asked myself at the time, 'Why is it that I feel more acceptable as "me" with these women whose beliefs and behaviour are very different from mine, than with some of the people at College who share my beliefs?' Now, I believe it was because they were more integrated as people. I was aware of a 'split' in me which I was struggling to reconcile, of which many at College were not even aware.

This was emphasised for me by an incident in my final year. At the carol service, Tom, one member of our year group, was performing a solo. The day before, he burst into the games room and threatened me with a snooker cue, accusing me of setting him up. I was clueless as to the source of his anger. It transpired that another student had put a message in his pigeonhole saying, 'Ring Mr C. Lion immediately about settlement at a potential church'. He did this only to discover he had rung London Zoo. The other student, having had enough of Tom 'setting up' others, had decided to repay him in kind. Tom promptly withdrew from the concert in protest at his treatment. What amazed me was that one of the best preachers in our year, who had been academically very successful and was generally regarded as a fine prospect as a church leader, had little insight into himself, or a sense of humour. On meeting Tom years later I recounted this incident, which we were both able to laugh at, so some things did change.

As I reflect back on this time at College I am aware of Jesus' teaching that it is perilously easy to spot flaws in others whilst being ignorant of even greater failings in oneself (Matt. 7:1–5). I was a confused twenty-two year old, struggling to understand myself, my wife and my God. What I learnt at College was both liberating in opening the new and exciting worlds of theology, psychiatry and psychotherapy, and painful in raising big questions about faith and life about which I had intuitive memories and feelings, without the vocabulary to describe them. I made important observations at that time that have both influenced the way I have perceived the Church, and shaped my development as a minister.

Firstly, the attitude modelled at College was very much 'You have come here to learn from us. We are the experts'. To some extent this was true. I needed to be taught theology and other related subjects. However, training is much more than the trans-mission of information. The time spent at theological college was intended as a training and preparation for ministry, which is much more than academic achievement. The unspoken assumptions passed on were to do with being in control. In transactional analysis terms there was a reinforcing of a parent-child model, where the parent is critical of the child wanting to become an adult. This is understandable to some extent in that living with adolescents can be a traumatic business. Adolescents need to push authority to the limit in order to discover their own emerging personality and identity. Perhaps time at theological college can be seen as a form of spiritual adolescence in the process of ministerial formation. College seemed to be totally unaware of this dynamic and they coped by becoming strong parents, holding firmly to their authoritarian role, without allowing the healthy process of adjustment that adolescents need.[4] I perceive this to be a very dangerous modelling for future ministry. Ministers thus trained might treat their congregations in the same way – 'We have the knowledge, we are preachers of God's authoritative Word'. This is a tremendously powerful and potentially abusive position to be in as I was to discover in my first church.

Secondly, following on from above, power was clearly invested in the structures of the College. If anyone questioned these or other unspoken norms, such as student representatives serving on the College council but being expected to say nothing, then it was made clear that this was 'inappropriate'. If one persisted then one was labelled as a 'trouble-maker' or 'difficult'. When I made comments at the College council meetings (not all of which were helpful), I was soon put in my place by other council members. This left me with a strong abhorrence of tokenism. I shall return to and discuss in detail in a later chapter power structures and dynamics at all levels of theological college life. These attitudes I saw as a clear contradiction of the nonconformist history and nature of the Baptist denomination. Indeed, the precedent goes much further back than that to numerous Old Testament prophets and to a certain founder of the Christian faith. He certainly didn't make it easy for those in power in his day.

Thirdly, we push away or defend ourselves from the things that we are afraid of. Much of the competitive nature of my year group, whether it was the number of books we possessed, what piece of camera equipment we had purchased or our latest mark for an essay, was about being afraid – afraid that we would not be good enough; afraid that we would not fit in; afraid that we would not be taken seriously, a ministerial 'lightweight'. One student left College after three years of the four-year course, having decided he did not want to go into the ministry. He was described as immature; his fiancée was blamed for diverting him from God's calling; he was seen as weak; he was accused of letting down the churches that had supported him through College. If anything, it took more courage for him to confront the issue and face the consequences by admitting he had made mistakes, rather than simply carrying on along the production line. I met up with him by accident on holiday recently for the first time in a decade. He was enjoying life as a solicitor and attending an Anglican church but interestingly he was still wrestling with whether or not he had made the right decision. The forces that come to bear when someone does something we may have thought about but find too uncomfortable to dwell on for any length of time, are frightening. So where in this College that believed God's Word, was there the outworking of 'There is no fear in love. But perfect love drives out fear because fear has to do with punishment' (1 John 4:18), or of 'My grace is sufficient for you, for my power is made perfect in weakness'? (2 Cor. 12:9) 'Weakness' was a word I never heard at College, yet it was commonplace in the worlds of psychiatry and psychotherapy to which I had been introduced at this time. In these worlds an acknowledgement of weakness was understood to be a desirable development rather than something to be defended against or denied.

Fourthly, there is an appalling danger in the Church, especially in the evangelical tradition, of 'splitting' between theory and practice and between good and bad. We affirm the good and deny the bad. We work hard at clarifying the theory and in doing so somehow assume that practice will just happen. Real life has a way of blasting holes, like rock from a quarry, in our careful archaeological dug-out theology. The term 'theological reflection' was not then in use but, as a means of linking or integrating the two, it has been a vital and healthy development in the field of pastoral theology.[5] This theme is so important that it emerges again and again in later chapters. It has its genesis for me here in the struggle to hold onto both the very good and the very bad aspects of College.

The 'good' lay in introducing me to a fully Trinitarian theology, in a way that I understood and with which I felt safe. I could now own God as Father, Son and Spirit in a unified and non-split manner that has been a foundation of my theological thinking ever since. It has enabled me to appreciate the work of a range of theologians including von Balthasar. He speaks of the Trinity in this way,

> the one God is, in his essence, love and surrender. Jesus knows, and acknowledges, himself to be the Word, Son, expression, and self-surrender – bearing witness to itself in love – of that Origin prior to which no existent is thinkable and which he calls the 'Father,' who loves him and whom he loves in common, divine Spirit of love, a Spirit whom he bestows upon us so we can be drawn into this abyss of love (vast beyond measure) and thus comprehend something of its superabundance: 'to know the love which surpasses knowledge' (Eph. 3:19).[6]

I was and still am captivated by that phrase 'the abyss of love' to describe my Triune God, especially as I was later to enter into the abyss of others' traumatic experiences. In their abyss of pain and abandonment there was still the possibility of encountering the abyss of God's presence and love.

The 'bad' was the lack of pastoral care for individuals in their own development or, like Mike and Julie, in their crisis situations.

At this stage of my Christian, ministerial and personal development, my primary quest was for integrity. Sadly, and it seems a harsh thing to say, this was lacking at College. I am aware that if I (as I think I and others were) was working through a spiritual adolescence, it would be easy to fall into the trap of denigrating parental figures.[7] Honesty compels me to say that I and others think and feel that this lack of integrity genuinely existed and is not simply the product of my emergent psycho-spiritual psyche. However I was impressed when at a later stage I met and talked with the Principal and mentioned how difficult I had found some of our encounters, he was honest enough to admit that he had misunderstood me. He was under enormous pressure at the time and it later transpired he was suffering from a difficult to diagnose medical condition that caused great pain. He also had a similar conversation with Mike, acknowledging that he had handled the situation badly at the time and wished it could have been otherwise. His attitude spoke to me of integrity, and I have tried to follow his example since starting ministry at my first church which is the subject of the next chapter.

5

⚹

THE PAIN AND POWER OF MINISTRY

The golden gleaming spire pointed heavenwards against a brilliant blue sky. God had provided superb weather for my first day as minister of my new church. I came secure in the knowledge that this was where God wanted me to be, notwithstanding a degree of pragmatism that this was the only church that had approached me. My colleague, the senior minister, welcomed me warmly and prayed that God would help us to work together to enable the church to be a vital part of God's kingdom. I had been attracted to the church partly by this man's public praying. As he led worship I thought, 'Here is someone I can learn from'. Another factor had been that the church, represented by the deacons, had shown a clear desire to help me grow and develop as a minister. My role involved co-ordinating youth work, encouraging evangelism, developing nurture groups for new Christians, preaching twice a month – my colleague said defensively to me that 'The people didn't want him out of his pulpit' – and 'sharing in the totality of church life and ministry'. We soon settled into a routine of meeting on Monday mornings to talk and pray together. One factor which became apparent very quickly was that my colleague had very fixed ideas. By 'evangelism' he meant his idea of evangelism, which I found to be a somewhat stilted American-style approach. My idea that the church develop a 'parish' (many members lived some distance away from the church) was dismissed. My suggestion that we alter the style of the services, making them less formal, using drama and various forms of musical instruments other than the piano and organ, and encouraging congregational participation was regarded as 'unworkable'. There were bound to be tensions between a new minister fresh from college and an older minister who had never worked with another minister before. At this stage, because he did not tell me, I did not realise that he had had a very tough time with some strong-minded and difficult deacons who, thankfully, had left before I arrived.

Monday mornings became a good-natured 'battle' over many areas of church life. I did learn from my colleague's experience and he did 'mellow' and allow some changes to take place. I also learned by what my colleague did not do – and that was to confront difficult situations. It was a time of growth for me and an appraisal after two years by the minister and church leaders noted that my preaching had improved, that I was easy to talk and relate to, that I encouraged people, that I had won the friendship, trust and respect of the young people, and that I had shown wisdom and taken time and trouble in persevering with difficult people. It was also noted that 'Alistair steps into situations too quickly and without tact and on occasions raises people's hackles' as well as 'attempting too much'. One church leader suggested that I should concentrate on counselling rather than anything else, as this was obviously what I was most skilled at. The minister disagreed and said that people should primarily relate to him.

Counselling came to feature more and more in my work. I began to build on the experience of being counselled, having discovered an intuitive feel for this area and having led groups both at theological college and in a psychiatric hospital (the two were not dissimilar). This was done both experientially and theoretically. I attended several counselling courses, one of which led to my joining an ongoing study/supervision group led by a Christian psychotherapist, Myra Chave-Jones, with which I remained for ten years. I also continued to work at Claybury on a one-day-a-week basis which continued my experiential training in group therapy and one of the chaplains provided supervision for the counselling I was doing. As part of my probationary studies for the Baptist Union I had chosen to read the original, unabridged version of Frank Lake's *Clinical Theology*, all 1200 pages! If I'm honest I skim read much of it and at that stage did not grasp all that I was reading. Yet it did continue to open up the worlds of psychiatry, psychotherapy, psychoanalysis and theology. My written work for these studies was 'A Christian evaluation of Sigmund Freud', which introduced me to Freud's actual writings, rather than other people's summaries of his ideas. This resulted in the suggestion that I pursue some further academic study, an idea that lay dormant for a few years. By now I had acquired a theoretical knowledge of psychoanalysis and other forms of psychotherapy and an experiential knowledge of group therapy and psychodrama. This was allied to developing skills as a pastoral counsellor and a combination of prayer and counselling called 'inner healing'. An increasing number of people, from both my own church and others, came to see me. This led to a confrontation with my colleague, who felt that I was spending too much time counselling and not enough doing evangelism. He was right, according to my job description, but made no allowances for other developments in my growth as a minister. My colleague made few concessions and this pattern of relating was to become the context of a much greater confrontation.

I had been invited by an American Southern Baptist minister to pastor his church in Morocco for four months. People in the church with a particular interest in mission were keen I should go, as was I. My colleague said 'no' and made it clear that there was to be no discussion on this matter. He dismissed my request without any real consideration and made me feel like a naughty schoolboy for even asking. We had a stand-up, face to face argument, where I felt any relationship of equality we had been working on was demolished as effectively as a wooden shack hit by a hurricane.

In stark contrast to this feeling of powerlessness in my own church with my senior colleague, I was invited to give the experience of my insight into group dynamics and counselling in another church. The leadership team valued me by asking me to help them face a difficult situation. The voice on the telephone sounded strained as the minister asked to see me at his home that evening about an urgent matter. He told me that he had also invited the associate minister. My mind ran through a whole range of possible scenarios as a way of coping with a mounting sense of anxiety.

The atmosphere in his home was tense as we walked through the hall into the lounge and were asked to sit down. There and then he said he was going to offer his resignation to the church. We were stunned – I had certainly not expected this. What could we say? In this tense, emotionally charged situation I was filled with sadness to see a strong man speaking through his tears and pain. There was a natural instinct to reach out and support such vulnerability – which we did. The associate minister went into the kitchen to have a talk with his wife as I sat there in raw silence, like a priest in a confessional box as he told his story. By now the room was in darkness as neither of us had moved to switch a light on. I heard about the utter loneliness of this man who ultimately had made ministry his consuming passion and failed to give to others the time they so desperately needed.[1] Later we gathered together to pray asking God to help in a situation where hurt, betrayal and self-deception had all played their part for a long time.

In the meantime it was 'business as usual' in my church – which consisted of my colleague continuing to give me a 'hard time' over some change I wanted to make. I was still angry with his categoric refusal to discuss even the possibility of me going to Morocco. Why was I so angry? In part it was the past catching up with me. Sometime earlier it dawned on me how like my father my colleague was. Had my feeling this was the right church for me been partly induced by an unconscious transference on my part, in which I viewed my colleague and my relationship with him, as one that made up for the relationship that I did not experience with my father? I think so. My anger was therefore about being let down by yet another 'father figure'. Another part of my anger was caused by the recollection of all the times my colleague had taken an authoritarian role that I had to do what I was told because he was 'right' and had had more experience of these matters than I. It transpired that my colleague had purposely been keeping me at a distance since an earlier incident when I had been alerted to a problematic relationship in the church through exercising a 'word of knowledge' (one of the spiritual gifts mentioned by the apostle Paul in I Corinthians 12). In this pastoral area he felt that I was taking over his role and challenging his authority, a factor he found particularly uncomfortable as it later transpired that he was planning to retire early, hence his insistence that I not be away from the church for any length of time.

Events at this other local church rolled on slowly and relentlessly like some out-of-control Chieftain tank, demolishing, crushing and bruising many in its path. Although the associate minister had refused to accept his colleague's immediate resignation, it was not ultimately his decision; the other church leaders had to consider the matter before bringing a recommendation to a meeting of all church members for a final decision. The church leaders recommended that his resignation be accepted. They took the view that while none of us are without sin,

> People not only inside the church, but outside it, believe rightly that in the way of life of an ordained minister they ought to be able to see a pattern which the church commends . . .Restrictions on what the clergy do stem from the pastoral function . . .their lives must be free from anything which will make it difficult for others to have their confidence in them as messengers, watchmen and stewards of the Lord.[2]

It was the associate minister's unenviable responsibility to guide this meeting in a manner which allowed room for people's shock, anger, grief and shattered illusions. Some sought to blame and condemn, others wanted everything 'swept under the carpet', others just cried, and all felt responsible in some unfathomable and self-blaming way. The result of the meeting was that the church believed it should accept the minister's resignation. The members acknowledged that given the right support this man could profitably have a ministry elsewhere, but that, given the length of time the situation had lasted, his ministry had ended in this church.

This was the start of a traumatic year. Suddenly I found myself leading my own church (as my colleague had now taken up his early retirement), yet being drawn into help in this tragic situation of the other church where the associate minister was now my friend. I was now preaching much more often (and consequently needing more time to prepare), maintaining the ongoing life of the church, coping with the intrusive speculation and gossip that I encountered at every turn as people believed that I knew the 'real' story of the other church and managing the resignation of two senior church leaders who objected to the more modern style I was introducing. My counselling skills were used as I listened to member after member in the other church disclosing how much they had invested in one fallible human being, little different from myself or any other minister. It reminded me of the chapter title in Howard Snyder's book *New Wineskins. Changing the man-made structures of the Church* which had been a big influence in shaping my vision for the Church. The chapter is called 'Must the Pastor be a Superstar?' He writes (with some amendment of his transatlantic language and culture),

> Meet the Reverend Jones, Superstar. He can preach, counsel, evangelise, administrate, conciliate, communicate and some-times even integrate. He can also increase the offering and church attendance. He handles Sunday morning better than any game-show host. He is better with words than most political candidates. As a scholar he surpasses many university professors. No church social function would be complete without him.

The caricature is real enough to hurt because my experience is that the church still looks for this kind of person to be their minister. They invest in this person their hopes, dreams, faith and fantasies, in effect making the minister a substitute god. The Evangelical Church that for centuries (on theological grounds) has reacted negatively to any kind of priestly role for clergy, can, if it is not careful, invest them instead with a very powerful psycho-logical role every bit as dangerous as an exaggerated view of priesthood. This comes about because of the presence of what Anna Freud called 'defence mechanisms' that form part of a hier-archy of coping styles that are expressed in relationships with others.[3] These are commonly thought of as being immature, neur-otic or unhelpful in relationships. Their value is that they keep the threat (whatever form that threat takes) at a safe distance and maintain our fragile sense of self, our ego. Michael Jacobs uses a medical analogy to describe their operation.

> In transplant surgery one of the major problems is the body's rejection of alien tissue; drugs are necessary to keep at bay the natural defences of the body, but at the same time they must not render the body so defenceless that there is a risk of infection. The mind has similar defences . . .employed in the face of unpleasant or shocking thoughts and feelings.[4]

I view the goal of all relationships to be the experience of love and intimacy.[5] This requires the ability to trust, risk and become vulnerable. There are times, in our pursuit of love and intimacy, when we experience the world and our nexus of relationships as threatening, almost overwhelming. On these occasions we protect ourselves in various psychological ways by what has been called 'defence mechanisms'. They protect us for a time, until we are more able to risk and trust once more. Thus we refashion our lives. Theologically, such a process reminds me of God's shaping of us as a potter fashions clay to produce a textured, three-dimensional object reflecting craftsmanship, beauty and the intrinsic qualities of the clay (Isa. 64:8; Jer. 18:6; Rom. 9:21). It reminds me, too, of St Paul's injunction to 'Work out your salvation with fear and trembling' (Phil. 2:12).

So defence mechanisms can have a healthy outcome. But because they are not acknowledged or recognised in the Church, they become ingrained patterns of behaviour in the relationship between the minister and the church members, often leaving both parties behind battlements, engaged in siege warfare. A commonly observed psychological defence is that of idealisation. It is said of a minister going to a new church that for the first year they can do nothing wrong, for the next year they can do nothing right, for the next year there is a stalemate while the minister looks for another church and once he or she leaves, they become the best minister the church ever had. The minister is seen as perfect, even like a god or goddess, and of course such beings are perfect. Problems with this dynamic arise in two ways. First, the person who idolises the minister (it happens to other authority figures such as doctors) is unable to recognise the person's shortcomings, fallibility and humanness. When finally these become apparent as they did with the minister in this case, the feeling of being 'conned' or 'let down' produces an explosive anger which is either turned on oneself and can produce depression or explodes outwards, the shrapnel hurting any innocent bystanders in the vicinity. I cannot count the hours I spent listening to people as they surveyed the 'bombed out' remnants of their faith, angry that they had been betrayed, and feeling stupid that they had allowed one person so to influence their faith. But, as with many emotional wounds when properly treated, the consequence was a more rooted and rugged faith. Being 'properly treated' meant developing a 'holding process',[6] along with other carers in the church, that facilitated a rediscovery of God.

Every minister can tell a story of at least one member who has become compulsively attached to them and made life very difficult. One woman used to ring a colleague up repeatedly and just breathe down the phone. When it finally became clear who was phoning, she said she did it just to hear his voice and that was all she needed. Every week there are people who project onto ministers their desires and dreams, finding in their fantasies an answer to their loneliness, an outlet for their sexuality, an expression of love from what they see as a 'safe' figure. Projection 'describes the way in which we ascribe to someone else a feeling or characteristic which is (also) our own, but which we do not apparently acknowledge as ours'.[7] A psychotherapist who worked with many evangelical clients told me that I would be shocked at the sexual fantasies that go on between church members and their minister. This phenomenon derives from the non-availability of someone who is allowed to get close and with whom secrets can be shared. 'The experiences and the fantasies of his clients will span the whole range of human experience, making soap operas, novels and even psychiatric text books appear insignificant compared to the real life dramas which are played out before him'.[8] The emotional intimacy of ministry can be very powerful[9] and is easily subject to abuse.[10] Other fantasies about ministers are about their intelligence, their spirituality, their 'direct line' to God and above all their power. So often it is power, a theme to which we shall return, that fuels these fantasies. A second consequence, and this links with my reflections about the style of ministry modelled at the college where I was trained, is that the process of idealisation encourages and underlines the power and control aspects of ministry. This can be evident even in the content of preaching. There is enough honesty and integrity in the Bible to show many biblical characters 'warts and all' yet when preached about, members often only hear about the positive aspects of their character from which various spiritual lessons are drawn. Samson is often a figure of amusement who becomes a hero in the end rather than being seen as an immature, selfish, narcissistic, sexually-demanding body-builder. If he were living in present-day California, a television psychologist would be selling the principles of his life as 'Men who love too much'.[11]

Ministers are encouraged to collude with such idealisation from church members. Who encourages them? We ministers do, because we all want approval. I want people to like me even as they read this book. The danger is that when we are no longer being idealised we no longer 'feel' that we are being successful or 'good' as ministers. We then criticise or reproach the church when things go wrong, and blame or accuse the members of not being committed or spiritual enough. They in turn mirror the same criticisms of the minister – 'If only he were more Spirit-filled everything would be OK.' Mutual recrimination becomes the order of the day. How can we break out of this destructive and distorted cycle? I find James Houston's approach liberating. Rather than perpetuating an idealised view of ministry, Houston writes, 'After years of feeling useless and guilty . . .I learned another important truth: that God calls us to use our Achilles' heel, where we limp most, to lead us through natural weakness or woundedness of personality, to grow spiritually strong.'[12] Houston goes on to develop this idea in respect to prayer which he describes as 'The Transforming Friendship', combining insights from pastoral counselling and spiritual traditions through the centuries, allied to a warm, liberating evangelical faith.

Another cluster of defence mechanisms found in the relationship between a church and minister are those of repression, denial and splitting. All of us cope with some thoughts and feelings by repressing them. I did this with many of the more negative feelings

I had about my time at theological college (explored in chapter 4) for quite a few years. It somehow seemed disloyal and unchristian to acknowledge, far less explore, such feelings. So I repressed or denied them, although I managed to avoid the 'split' where theological college and the church were either 'good' or 'bad'. From my own experience therefore I can recognise traces of the operation of such psychological mechanisms in other church situations, when I talk with other church leaders or lecture at other theological or training colleges.

One issue that is repressed, denied and split in the Evangelical Church in particular is the whole area of sexuality. Interestingly many of the people who come wanting some form of therapeutic help are concerned about issues of sexuality – Christians bring unresolved issues relating to sexuality, often heavily repressed; and non-Christians, who have no problems at all with their sexuality and its physical expression, bring unresolved issues to do with intimacy and meaning. Fortunately this area is now being addressed by the Church, as is evidenced by these extracts from the foreword to a recent book about homosexuality.

> In the recent past, Christian writers on homosexuality ran the risk of falling into opposite traps. Some in a praiseworthy attempt to counter homophobia in church and society, have bypassed the Bible's negative approach to homosexual behaviour in order to affirm homosexual people. Others, angered by such a liberal evasion of Scripture, have condemned homosexual behaviour so harshly that any man or woman with a same-sex preference inevitably feels hopeless and marginalized . . . A simplistic approach to the relevant biblical teaching is being seriously challenged . . . The discipline of hermeneutics is asking vital questions about the way the Bible's teaching is interpreted and applied across the culture gap . . . The issue of homosexuality will not disappear because people with same-sex preferences will not go away. Nor should they. This book will deepen your understanding of your own humanity – and theirs.[13]

There is still a great deal of careful listening, thinking, and exploring to be done, and it will be possible only if the Church as a whole is facilitated by leaders who are able to encounter their own denial, repression and splitness, and model for their church community God's integrating work incarnated in fallible, fragile beings.

A third area of complication in this tangled relationship between church and minister, illuminated by defence mechanisms, is that of regression where there is a retreat into childlike patterns of behaviour. This can reinforce a view of the minister as an idealised parent who will come along and make things better, which again places him or her in a powerful position. If he or she is viewed as a parental figure (often a father as most ministers are male), another complex psychological process called transference is introduced. Church members transfer onto the minister all sorts of feelings and emotions relating to human fathers (good and bad) and they do the same thing to a heavenly Father (often perceived in the light of their experience of a human father). James Houston's difficulties in prayer, mentioned earlier, stemmed from his transferring onto God what he saw in his relationship with his father. This transference is not always bad. However, given the prevalence of sexual and other abuse, often initiated by men, it may be negative. I mentioned earlier that I realised how like my own father my colleague was. What happened in my relationship with the senior minister was a kind of parental dynamic, or in psychodynamic terms – an oedipal triangle[14] – where I competed with my parental colleague, as a new arrival, for the attention of the mother church. This, however, was not the only triangular relationship in which I became embroiled.

The consequences of the local minister's resignation unfortunately did not remain confined to the limited pastoral support I could offer to this betrayed and angry church community, struggling to understand, struggling to forgive and struggling to accept how God could have allowed this to happen. A church member, who knew she was dying, wanted 'her minister', who had now left, to come back and to take her funeral. The church agreed to this, since it occurred soon after his leaving, but it was made clear that it was only with the church's permission. Earlier, in an informal conversation, I had said, in an attempt to convey that he still had a future as a minister, that he ought to be able to do weddings and funerals at the church. However, within a short time the church leadership disagreed, realising that any continuing involvement would be unhelpful and actually hinder the grieving process the church was facing.

In a letter nine months after his resignation this minister was still 'fighting his corner' even though he had chosen to resign and had not been asked to resign by the Church. The letter illustrates most of the defence mechanisms I mentioned earlier – denial, repression, splitting, and projection. It was and still is, if I allow it to be, a bullying and abusive letter, and betrays little or no under-standing of the pain he precipitated in the church. For nine months his colleague and I had struggled to hold together and lead a traumatised group of people. Some days I struggled to keep myself going as I wrestled with my own church and the issue of power. I was told information about this minister, which, had it been made public, would have destroyed any good memories that people were holding onto. Yielding to the temptation to hit back would in reality have been as abusive to him as he had been to me and his colleague. I learned through this incident the way in which abuse perpetuates abuse, and the terribly seductive and attractive nature of power. What stopped me was the straightforward inter-vention of God. The Bible told me that such an action was wrong and would be sinful, and it was a route I chose not to follow. I was greatly helped in my spiritual and emotional struggles by one individual and two groups. Keith had become a friend just before I started at theological college and as an older minister subsequently became my advisor whilst I was a probationary minister. His counselling insight, his pastoral wisdom, his willingness to 'feel' with me in the injustice of the situation, his allowing of my anger to be a real un-split-off part of me and his habit of dragging me to a pub for a drink gave me a lifeline when I thought it was all too much. I was also supported by a small group of ministers with whom I had met for lunch each week for the previous three years. Their love, patience and support was a profound help as was a group of Christian counsellors and psychotherapists with whom I met each month. Their objective insight and care was a resource that enabled me to continue with fresh insight into myself and the ways in which God was at work. I did make mistakes. I did keep too much to myself and become too involved in this other church situation. I did break a confidence (one of only two occasions) which rightly incurred the anger of the person involved. At that time I rationalised what I had done. Several years later when the wound caused by this time had begun to heal, I realised how badly I had let this person down, so I went to see him to apologise and say I was sorry. He did say I had let him down but still valued me as me anyway, even more so now I had had the courage to face the truth of what had happened.

Even now I recoil at the pain of this time. To feel so alone, so defenceless and vulnerable, so powerless, despite a caring, supportive wife and great friends, had a scarring effect on my inner being. My face carries a few small scars from my motorcycle accident but these are nothing to the emotional wounds that were inflicted. Yet I can see now in the paradox of God's grace, they were to become resources that brought healing to others. In facing my own pain again and living with it I could help others live with theirs. As I reflected on this chapter I came to realise that I had never really forgiven the minister whose church I had tried to help. I had let the events lose their painful ability to hurt but I had not erased the wound itself. I understood in theory but not in practice. Yet I can now say that these recollections have unleashed painful memories that I can today let rest. I have worshipped at the idol of innocent hurt long enough. I do not view this struggle to forgive as failure. It has enabled me to live in the same territory as others whose abuse has been so much more painful than my own. I understand their long, long struggle to forgive and allow healing to begin.

This time at my first church taught me a great deal about myself and about others. I had developed counselling skills that were to be further enhanced, little knowing that the church which sought to develop skills in me would be the place where many of them were to be used. I had started some further academic study on Frank Lake and the importance of Clinical Theology for pastoral theology. I had helped another church through a stormy and traumatic time, not so much by my strong, macho leadership, as modelled at theological college, but rather by a recognition of power and both a choosing to 'own' its appeal to me and being able to avoid using it to get what I wanted. A crucial ability to do this came through a process of self-awareness worked at by me in my time at Claybury and with Keith. This contrasted with the conventional image of leadership, which I see as fraught with danger. To have skills of leadership, teaching, preaching, caring and worship leading, yet to fail to explore what is going on in oneself and to delve into the psychological and emotional aspects of ministry, is a dangerous path. The danger lies in an inability to recognise the presence of powerful, un-owned, unacknowledged and often unconscious emotions and feelings.

A few people, when they became aware of the situation at this neighbouring church and knew I had been involved in helping, shared with me similar experiences in which they had been involved. The message is stark, that the church tradition to which I belong and want to affirm, cannot pretend that all is well. The fact that a person has right doctrine says nothing about his or her ability to live a right life. If Freud is right that the value of religion and 'its power lies in the truth which it contains',[15] then the more honest, the more real, the more truthful the Church can be, the better. I discovered that people do not always want the truth about themselves or others, and to face a part of the Church with such observations results in rejection and avoidance. One friend has risked expressing his ideas in a stimulating and thought-provoking book, *The Radical Evangelical*.[16] Yet this has been reviewed by an influential evangelical organisation in a critical way. 'What this book represents is certainly radical. There is reason to doubt, however, whether it can be called evangelical in any meaningful way.'[17] Like other evangelicals,[18] I was beginning to discover that to face the truth about what we honestly felt and thought was likely to result in being pushed to one side – pushed towards exile, into that no-person's land.

6

❧

INTO THE ABYSS

My imagination roamed over the bleak and barren topography of Bodmin Moor on a journey towards the Jamaica Inn.

> It seemed to her that never before had she known there was malevolence in solitude. The very coach, which all day had rocked her like a cradle, now held a note of menace . . . the showers of rain, increasing in violence . . . spat against the windows with new venom. On either side of the road the country stretched interminably into space. No trees, no lanes, no cluster of cottages or hamlet, but mile upon mile of bleak moorland, dark, untraversed, rolling like a desert land to some unseen horizon. No human being could live in this wasted country, thought Mary, and remain like other people; the very children would be born twisted, like the blackened shrubs of broom, bent by the force of the wind that never ceased . . . Their minds would be twisted, . . . their thoughts evil, dwelling as they must amidst marshland and granite, hard heather and crumbling stone . . . On wound the road across the dark and silent land, with never a light to waver for an instant as a message of hope.[1]

The incessant ring of the telephone interrupted my imagining and brought me back to reality like some slowly deflating balloon. 'I need a favour', Mark said. 'Would you be willing to see someone I have been trying to help but feel that I am out of my depth with?' Mark knew that I had worked in a psychiatric hospital, had spent time counselling others and felt that Rachel needed some kind of 'inner healing',[2] but precisely why or in what area he could not say. I agreed to meet with Rachel and Mark, but can recall little of the meeting, apart from my thinking, 'This person needs more help than a few quick prayers'. When I left I said that I would be willing to see her again and explore what might be the problem. Shortly afterwards Rachel contacted me to see if something could be arranged, so we agreed to meet where she worked as a youth worker.

Rachel walked into the room and sat down. I noted her blue eyes, her highlighted hair, her use of a small amount of make-up, her faded blue jeans and her white cotton blouse, which were in contrast to her previous black attire. Her face had a warm quality to it, I saw the glimpse of a smile and a glint in her eye. I was not sure what the glint was about but when I talked to her, she looked away and staring at the ground, avoided looking at me most of the time. All I did was listen. Listen to her sadness and pain as she recalled the death of her mother and her guilt at not being there when she had died. She now felt depressed and alone. Her mother meant so much to her (her father having died when she was a teenager) that she had desperately wanted to be there. Rachel blamed herself. I thought, 'Why is she being so hard on herself?' It seemed to me that there was a good deal more to the situation, and I asked if I could see her again. The next time we met the focus was on her depression and how she was feeling.[3] I noted almost intuitively (the clues being provided by her very controlled and contained outward appearance) that she was angry. Near the end of the session I said, 'You seem to be angry about something.' Rachel shouted back, her face a clenched mask of pain, 'I'm not an angry person.' My response was, 'You seem angry to me.' We agreed to meet for an initial number of sessions to explore what was going on. Now, as a more experienced counsellor, I cringe at some of the 'mistakes' I made. I had not listened enough. My sense that she was angry (based on what I was feeling in me) could have been wrong and sidetracked Rachel, leaving her feeling that she had been 'labelled' and treated as some problem to be neatly disposed of. However, some unconscious process was at work whereby she felt that she could trust me. Her intuitive sense was that it would be all right to explore who she was with me, a comparative stranger. Neither of us knew at this stage that an important part of our backgrounds was the influence of both being fraternal twins. The psychoanalyst Neville Symington describes this process this way,

> The emotional upheaval of the first encounter changes the two participants, who will never be the same people again. I also believe that a new entity is forged; a new reality emerges. The two people do not remain independent entities . . . In the analytic encounter . . . there is an instant fusing so that the new being emerges.[4]

Only later was I to discover what a profound risk Rachel had taken and what a profound gift she had given me. One theory is that people brought up in competitive families or with possessive mothers learn the ability to detect minute psychological changes, so that it becomes an inherent skill, almost an unconscious means of communication, an idea that Skynner also mentions concerning his training of family therapists.[5] Competitive influences on me, dating from conception, perhaps gave me some dimly understood but all-too-real insight into this hurting person. I was right, Rachel was angry. The early sessions became an open-ended contract of weekly and, for a year, twice weekly sessions that stretched over a total of three years. We worked on what was current in Rachel's life, often exploring her frequent and gruesome nightmares. Whatever was happening consciously her unconscious was producing terrifying images of Nazi death camps, decomposing bodies and other graphic and shocking images. This was also complicated by her faith in God, which left her feeling a total failure. I knew something of this as it, too, had been part of my spiritual journey, so there was an empathetic bond concerning a Father God who was distant and remote. Rachel was convinced that God could not possibly love a person who was as 'disturbed' as she was. She had tried all the usual evangelical remedies – being a committed, prayerful, Bible-reading Christian, a member of a Charismatic church where she had been 'ministered to' but all to no avail. One week we touched on the passage in Luke 11:11–12 which talks about a father giving good gifts to his children: 'Would any of you who are fathers give your son a snake when he asks for a fish? Or would you give him a scorpion when he asks for an egg?'

Rachel replied, 'Fathers always give scorpions, that's what they are meant to do.' Until this stage Rachel had focused exclusively on her mother, her depression and her nightmares. Here, after six months, as we spoke of fathers for the first time, we uncovered a seething mass of poisonous snakes inducing a paralysing fear, as if we were facing the hypnotic movement of a cobra about to strike its intended victim with a deadly venomous bite. Rachel found herself helpless, but not alone. It was another spiral in what was to be, and I use the word carefully, a descent into the hell of another's experience. Dante, the twelfth-century Italian poet, describes it well.

> Halfway through our trek in life
> I found myself in this dark wood,
> miles away from the right road.
> It's no easy thing to talk about,
> this place, so dire and dismal
> I'm terrified just remembering it!
> Death itself can hardly be worse;
> but since I got some good there
> I'll talk about the bad as well.[6]

Rachel and I were about to enter a dark, volcanic, uncharted abyss which threatened to erupt, spewing molten lava on all in its path. Twice a week for fifty minutes at a time we embarked on an emotional journey whose path took us to places of utter blackness, all-consuming rage, tortuous pain, denial, and depressive and destructive anger. The innovative psychiatrist and pastoral theologian, Frank Lake, talks in detail about 'the abyss of non-being'.[7] Others talk of the darkness of God's apparent abandonment and spiritual desolation with no light to guide.[8] This theme resonates with the dark night of the soul written about by St John of the Cross, the seventeenth-century Spanish mystic. He talks about two darknesses: the first of these purges the senses or desires and is 'bitter and terrible'; the second, and much rarer, experience purges the spiritual in preparation for a divine union of love that is to come. In the meantime one faces what is 'horrible and awful'.[9] The descriptions that best make sense of my feelings from this time, which have not been easy to access, are some of the intensely personal and moving passages in Brian Keenan's *An Evil Cradling*, his shatteringly painful account of captivity and torture in Beirut. It dawned on me that in this journey I was less of a guide and more a bodyguard, alert to potential life-threatening danger and attempting to minimise the risks. I was simply a presence, yet this in itself is enough, to 'be' with another.

> Presence is a service of vulnerability. To be present to others is to put oneself in a position of being vulnerable to what they are vulnerable to, and of being vulnerable to them. It means being willing to suffer what the other suffers, and to go with the sufferer in his or her own suffering . . . Presence does not involve taking another's place. That would be demeaning. It would suggest, 'I can take your suffering better than you can, so move aside, I will replace you.' Instead, presence involves exposing oneself to what the sufferer is exposed to, and being with the other in that vulnerability.[10]

How did I learn to be present in this way? Lake suggests, 'The pastor is compelled to tap the deepest roots of his own experience, or confess himself empty', his task, like that of Buber's psychotherapist, 'is to be the watcher and healer of sick souls'; who 'again and again confronts the naked abyss.'[11] How was this ability born in me? I sense now that being a twin has meant that I have always had a capacity for a companionship, a presence in depth with another, that is distinct from the complementarity of a sexual partner. This enabled me to journey with Rachel, even though any pain that I had experienced paled into insignificance as we encountered hers. Similarly my recent experiences of pain and rejection through trying to help out a colleague's church had left a deep scar. Yet the word scar can also mean 'a bare craggy rock formation'.[12] I was to discover a psychological granite in me and in my faith in God, experienced metaphorically as the 'Rock'. God is described as the Rock (Gen. 49:24; II Sam. 22:2; Ps. 18), the source of all strength and power and the ground of all confidence (which echoes Tillich's phrase 'the ground of all Being'). On this rock and through the Rock there comes about divine revelation (Judg. 6:20–1, 13:19), a numinous, awe-inspiring communion between God and person. It also serves as a symbol of firmness and resolution (Isa. 50:7; Ezek. 3:9).[13] In the depths of another one can encounter the source of that person's being and the revealing, shalom-bringing presence of God, which together provide a numinous experience of resolution. This is easier to understand after the event than in the event itself.

This experience had a profound effect on my theological understanding. It took me to a place where theology had no answer at that moment. My head told me of the all-encompassing presence of God and this meant that he must have been in the abyss. Yet his presence was hidden, shadowed, suffering in utter identification, allowing the Spirit of God, 'he who searches our hearts' (Rom. 8:27), to work 'with groans that words cannot express' (8:26) to guide my unconscious intuition along these rarely travelled paths. This theme is taken up by Matthew Fox in his thought-provoking book *Original Blessing*,[14] echoing Macquarrie's idea of original righteousness.[15] Fox suggests that the growth of the human person takes place in the dark underground, in subterranean passages. There, where,

> No image has ever reached into the soul's foundations, God alone works . . . The way of the unconscious mind . . . is the way of darkness. The depths of our beings are not at all sunlit; to see clearly, we must be willing to dive into the dark, inner abyss and acknowledge the creatures we may find there. How does one learn to discover the darkness and to befriend it again?[16]
>
> . . . Pain . . . empties us, if we allow it . . . Pain is everywhere − deep, ineffable, unfathomable, cosmic pain. Facing the darkness, admitting the pain, allowing the pain to be pain is never easy. This is why courage . . . is the most essential virtue of the spiritual journey. But if we fail to let pain be pain . . . the pain will haunt us in nightmarish ways. We will become pain's victims instead of the healers we might become.[17]

Fox expands further how this painful spiritual journey can help us to become healers of others.

First, pain helps us to understand other people in pain . . . it is eminently shareable . . . Secondly, pain . . . sensitizes us to what is truly beautiful in life . . . unwished for pain, provided we pray it or enter into it and do not cover it up and run from it, can often bring that love of life back to us . . . A third way in which pain enlivens us . . . [is] . . . It makes us stronger by testing us and demanding discipline of us that we did not know we were capable of . . . Sensitivity, which includes sensitivity to pain, also demands strength . . . the strength that vulnerability is about.[18]

But where do God and faith fit into this picture?

Pain and suffering . . . can be so deep, so dark, so silent, so untouchable and so unresolvable that it can appropriately be called nothing. We touch the void in our pain . . . In biblical faith our trust extends even to nothingness. Our Creator is author of all things, even of nothingness. Our fall into nothingness can be and must be trusted . . . The dark night of our souls is a special occasion for divine birth and opportunity, provided we let the darkness be darkness and the nothing be nothing . . . The Creator God, a great underground river, awaits . . . God is already at home in a deep, deep way but we need to return home to make contact with that depth.[19]

In biblical terms, the Lord is a 'revealer of mysteries' (Dan. 2:47), who 'reveals deep and hidden things; he knows what lies in darkness, and light dwells with him' (Dan. 2:22) and who 'reveals the deep things of darkness and brings deep shadows into the light' (Job 12:22). My instinctive understanding was that God was at work, but in a way that my previous theological training had not allowed for. I recalled Psalm 139 with a dawning awareness that the searching of God and the presence of God were in both our inner and outer worlds, our conscious and our unconscious. Here in the darkness, where nothing is hidden from God, here in the depths, where God is already present, the door opened. The lock was stiff, the hinges rusted, and it could only be opened a crack at a time, revealing what was at the heart of the pain. 'My father abused me,' Rachel said. This proved to be the turning-point, the beginning of growth over the next two years, as Rachel focused her anger on another rather than on herself.

Each session we would begin with Rachel exploring her current struggle, knowing that I was the one person who truly knew the context in which this was being lived, without having to go through the whole story again – although there were times when we went back to those dark, destroying places, to see how these abusive experiences had shaped her life. Yet in the telling and re-telling of her 'story', in the acceptance of Rachel at her most fragile, in the void of blackness where she almost ceased to be, Rachel began to 'feel' something for her father. He was not just a monster, he was a real person struggling with his own mental health, capable of loving, unabusive acts, for her and others. Rachel began to remember good times, holidays, family events that brought laughter and happiness. She started to walk to the local park and regularly sat under a big, spreading tree that reminded her of a secure place where she used to hide as a child. Here, although still not convinced that he listened, she talked to God about her father. Her idea of God changed from that of a vengeful, destructive force, to a benign but distant force who could be approached through Jesus. Jesus and his acceptance of women as they were, recounted for us in the Gospels, gave Rachel hope. One day we both went to this tree to 'bury' her father. He had died when she was a teenager and she had not been present. The memories had haunted her until, in the company of another, she had been able to name these dark, shapeless and destructive forces, and she had not been destroyed. The threatened consequences of telling her secret had not been enacted. In this 'burial' we acknowledged the past and left it there.

During this time I asked myself many questions. Was I competent to deal with such issues? Was I out of my depth? If I stopped now, would Rachel feel betrayed? The answers I arrived at were 'yes' and 'no'. My competence as a counsellor working at this depth was unproven. I knew the theory (though I now recognise that I knew less theory than I thought I did) but was working this out in practice with this client. I have learnt in subsequent training as a counsellor how dangerous and potentially damaging such a time might have been. Yet this therapeutic relationship did work well. Irvin Yalom, an American psychotherapist, raises the same issue:

> The problem in therapy is always how to move from an ineffectual intellectual appreciation of truth about oneself to some emotional experience of it . . . How I long for the certainty that orthodoxy offers. Psychoanalysis . . . always posits such strong convictions about the necessary technical procedures – indeed, analysts seem more certain of *everything* than I am of *anything*. How comforting it would be to feel, just once, that I knew exactly what I'm doing in my psycho-therapeutic work . . . But, of course, it is all illusion . . . ideological schools with their complex metaphysical edifices succeed because they assuage the *therapist's* . . . anxiety (and thus permit the therapist to face the anxiety of the therapeutic process). The more the therapist is able to tolerate the anxiety of not knowing, the less need there is for the therapist to embrace orthodoxy. The creative members of an orthodoxy, *any* orthodoxy, ultimately outgrow their disciplines. Though there is something reassuring about an omniscient therapist who is always in control . . . there can be something power-fully engaging about a fumbling therapist . . . willing to flounder . . . until they together stumble on an enabling dis-covery.[20]

Part of my 'gift' to Rachel was a willingness to endure her pain, guided by my own, with a sense of being held in the knowledge and experience of God being God, paradoxically ever present even in absence, the source of all being even in nothingness. I had not yet acquired the theoretical suit of armour to protect me and part of this vulnerability communicated to Rachel. It is not without significance that this therapeutic relationship developed during the time I felt 'abused' by the colleague in whose church I had been asked to help (see chapter 5).

What did I learn as a result of this significant relationship with Rachel?

First, I learned to value the depths of pain that we all pass through, some far more than others. My own experiences gave me some glimpses of insight into Rachel's. Encountering pain, befriending it, living with it, become ways of discovering who one truly is. Brian Keenan demonstrates this in *An Evil Cradling*. The book became for him 'a kind of reflective symphony of incidents, feelings, words and thoughts.' I was to discover that I am someone who is able to contain the pain of others in a way that makes it safe for them, enabling them to discover new horizons for themselves. So often I see the care offered by others as being invasive and taking control. My pain has taught me how I would feel if such a kind of care were offered to me, I respect people too much to do that to them. What I have learnt to offer is a non-invasive care that holds others without any conscious exploitation. At times this is more costly than I dare to think, and operating as I now do, in a much more theoretically informed way, actually makes it harder to enter into that pain for others. Yet I have as my example Jesus, whom I try to follow.

Second, there are times in a therapeutic relationship where there are no fresh words, no new sounds, no illuminating ideas. The stark words of discovery, the painful wretched experience of previous rejection and betrayal remain. They linger, like some predatory animal hoping for an easy kill on a weakened victim. Silence envelopes like a fog, wrapping itself like a bandage around the eyes except this is no innocent game of blind man's bluff. This experience is mutual as there emerges a therapeutic symmetry. Does a client select a therapist because unconsciously there is a recognition of a mutuality of hidden wounds that remain unhealed? What are these hidden wounds? They were for me a realisation that I barely knew myself and this was one reason for entering into my own therapy at a later stage. There was much of me that was hidden despite my efforts to be open and honest, something my friends value in me. I sense that there is in all people an estranged loneliness which lies at the heart of personal relationships. From this inner place the search for meaning, value and relationships springs. My faith and belief in God are expressed in acknowledging this need and attempting its repair. For many others who reject this route, another way is found in psychotherapy which doesn't offer the same answer but offers another person to share in this painful journey of discovery. I have benefited from both and discovered that the journey to wholeness takes one to surprising places and to encounters with surprising people.

Third, in this therapeutic relationship with Rachel I had to confront my own feelings. Feelings of: a sense of power; wanting more information; of anger and frustration at being helpless; of despair about the Church and the way that it had let Rachel down; and of guilt in that I was an integral part of that same institution. There were also other painful and uncomfortable discoveries such as the fact that I was a man with the potential to abuse others, especially women.

The journey also meant acknowledging that there is an ability to hate and destroy in all of us. This was a particular discovery of Freud who turned the spotlight from 'out there' to 'in here', onto the drives within us – the origins of love and hate.[21] That each of us, with or without faith in God, can hate is an important discovery. Winnicott developed this idea further and said, 'However much he loves his patients he cannot avoid hating them and fearing them, and the better he knows this the less will hate and fear be the motives determining what he does to his patients.'[22] An examination of my own motives, my desires and the forces at work within me is of huge significance for my ability to help others. Until my relationships with Rachel and with the church colleague, I had been somewhat naive about the depths of love and hate in all of us. In a sense I 'grew up' at the cost of some innocence but in a way that was to provide inner resources at a depth I had not imagined before. My 'story' is summed up by some more words of Brian Keenan, 'During my captivity I . . .was forced to confront the man I thought I was and to discover that I was many people. I had to befriend these many people, discover their origins, introduce them to each other and find a communality between themselves and myself.'[23]

Fourthly, I realised that this relationship gave as much to me as it did to Rachel. Rachel began as a client and became a friend, a very close friend, which breaks all the therapeutic rules. Part of my joy was to see her grow and develop professionally and as a lovely human being, growth made all the more significant to me by our shared knowledge. I and very few others know the cost which she has faced to become who she is. Part of her joy is to be accepted as an equal, when she began by feeling very unequal. Yet there is more to it than that. In the course of writing this book, and asking Rachel to describe for herself what this time meant, I made fresh discoveries for myself. If I were to write Rachel a letter it might be like this.

Let me begin by thanking you for what you have given to me. This is so much more than the recent book and the numerous books and gifts down through the years. What began as a risky therapeutic encounter for both of us has developed into a friendship whose roots run deep and perhaps even more than that as I shall try and explain.

I think I am conscious now even more so than at any other time that my identity, my frustration and my searching arise out of being a twin – always bound, yet independent of – an other. Part of my drivenness and desire to succeed is a sense of having to demand people's attention since I was not always the natural focus of this because I was either in competition with my twin sister or we were referred to simply as 'the twins' thus losing our distinct identities. Interestingly the motto of clan Ross is 'success nourishes hope'.

So from the shared experience of, in my case, an emotionally absent but loving father and in your case, an emotionally and sexually abusive but loving father, there was an instinctive understanding that you could 'trust' me as an empathetic therapist who was not so overwhelmed by his own agenda as to exploit the fragilities of the therapeutic relationship. In a real sense you 'sensed' my pain without feeling that you had to take it into yourself. As I hung on and stayed with my pain (unknown to you there was, I now believe, a huge transference going on between myself and the minister in the other church that ended in a painful rejection for both of us) it enabled you to stay with yours. My recollection was that it took two years to really begin to explore the molten mass of your feelings. When I left the area it was sooner than I would have chosen for you therapeutically, but as a true survivor it was the time to launch your rather frail and leaky boat and to your amazement (and sometimes to mine) it sailed pretty well.

As time went on you traded that little boat for an ocean-going ship to sail the seas of your own memories and emotions and those of others. Our relationship changed and transformed or metamorphosed into an ability to celebrate and enjoy ourselves. At and around this time, particularly I think when you started professional training, the relationship moved to being a friendship with, I think, a competitive, sibling edge to it, something you noticed before me.

However, I feel this doesn't quite untangle or adequately explain what I feel for you. Words abound: friend, equal, colleague, someone who loves me and whom I love in turn. They are close but not close enough. It feels to me that in some indescribable way you have become part of me in the same way that my twin sister is a part of me. Research about twins suggests that some go through life yearning for a re-creation of that original relationship. If it is possible for there to be a sense of completeness about a relationship with another, then in an emotional sense that bond is there with you and what I feel about you. That does not mean that we are ultra close but that something has 'fused' creating this attachment that will always be around the nexus of relationships that we forge from now on. Perhaps we have encountered the twin in each other and formed a new psychological 'twinness' that has a feeling of wholeness for both of us.

The last thing I want to say is how much I value you as you. I feel very proud of the quality of the therapeutic work I did with you but I recognise that it was you who did the really hard work with a courage that I feel similarly proud about. And I also feel privileged that it has not stopped there. I am glad of our friendship and more for all the reasons I have mentioned above and because it was and is still an affirmation of trust in me that makes me feel 'special'.

I never dreamed that Rachel and her story would become such

an important part of my story. Her life, fragile and flawed as it was, like a valuable antique mirror, enabled me to see 'me' more fully than I had been able to see before. The next chapter is Rachel's story in her own words.

7

STAINED GLASS WINDOWS:
RACHEL'S STORY

I remember once reading that we remember best beginnings and endings – with what falls in between being the hardest to access. This seems true as I look back, from many years on, at the three years' counselling with Alistair. What has also surprised me is my reluctance, in some ways, to do so. It is as if that is a film from someone else's story which, like scenes which horrify us, I would prefer to distance myself from. Yet I am equally aware it *is* part of me and of my history which I need to own and to integrate. This latter is an ongoing task of which writing this will inevitably form a part.

I first met Alistair when he was called in by my church minister to talk with me. I think it was an act of semi-desperation on the minister's part, a sign of his recognition of reaching the end of his own resources, yet it is something I will always be grateful to him for. He had for some time been talking to me on an occasional basis as the result of my growing sense of depression and hopelessness. At the time I was in the employ of the church as a youth worker, which also made him in a sense my 'line manager' – a point I will return to later. There was no obvious precipitating factor, although my mother had died some two years earlier. However, I had seemed to grieve appropriately and there was nothing to account for the way I felt. The depression had begun slowly and a poem I wrote at the time accurately reflects the deepening sense of isolation.

The fog

At first unseen creeps the fog,
Lightly skipping over the soul,
Curling gently, clinging lightly,
Insidious first sign
Of the darkness to come.

Then sighted,
Thickening slowly over the heart,
Gripping more closely,
Encompassing firmly,
Emotions die as the darkness deepens.

Sight fails at last
Far objects – future – cannot be seen.
Only the eerie silence
Thoughts and memories
Mingled in swirling confusion.
The isolation is complete.

A normally lively and vivacious person, I had continued to engage in all my church activities and only one friend was aware of my feelings, but there was an inner sense of my emotions dying and a growing sensation of loneliness. I did not feel able to share this with other church members for a number of reasons. One of these was a sense of shame which emanated from my own background, where feelings were not acknowledged and expression of them unheard of, though I was not aware of this at the time. What I was aware of was that there seemed to be a view – implicit rather than explicit – in the church that there were those who were 'strong' – including those in the employ of the church and the elected leaders – and those who were 'needy'. Those in need of help or ministry were seen as not yet ready for working in the church. This I felt came partly from the previous minister, a strong leader with many gifts who inspired a similar rather macho kind of leadership style in others. The new minister was more open to a sense of humanity and vulnerability but it seemed that at a subconscious level the split remained. I was therefore convinced (rightly or wrongly) that were I to admit my sense of struggle I would be disqualified from working within the church setting. This work was important to me not least because it gave some structure to my week amid an ever-increasing sense of inner panic and chaos.

I can still remember the first words Alistair ever said to me. We were sitting in my minister's study – both he and the minister sitting some distance from me. The desperation that meant I would try anything was in conflict with the sense of apprehension at being with these two men. I had a level of trust in my minister, however, which meant that by 'proxy' I had a level of trust in Alistair. This was to be sorely tested in the future. It was also tested then when his first words to me were, 'Do you always wear black?' I was dressed in black on that occasion, but felt insulted at the implication that it reflected something about me. In retrospect, it was probably more symbolic than I was prepared to acknowledge then.

This first meeting consisted of my saying a little about my history and how I had been feeling, and the two men praying for me in an inner healing style. This meant praying and imagining Jesus present. I cannot remember much detail, except that they were asking me to imagine being in a room (I think, however, that I remember it as a prison). Jesus was in the room with me. This filled me with terror. Remembering it now I recall a huge confusion over whether it was Jesus or my father there – so much so I'm not sure which they asked me to visualise. However, I can remember the fear – paralysing, suffocating fear which I knew meant that Jesus must not get near me. I would rather be alone in my room/prison than be close to him. I had been a Christian for some fourteen years, so I was deeply confused by this. My theoretical beliefs that he could be trusted battled with a stronger set of unconscious feelings. I can still remember the gentleness with which both Alistair and my minister treated me – almost as if they sensed the fragility of my inner world, which I, too overwhelmed by the intensity of my feelings, could not sense or express.

At the end of the time Alistair said goodbye and mentioned that the minister had his address should I need it. I've often wondered what prompted that remark, seemingly made in passing. I thought, 'No chance! I'll be fine'! I listened to their whispering as Alistair left and wondered what on earth he was saying about me. I had been grateful for his sense of compassion, but my whole life I had been a coper. I was the kind of person to whom others instinctively turned in difficulty and whom others perceived as strong and capable. I had no wish for people to see me in so vulnerable a state, and had allowed my minister to do so only because I was terrified of the sense of falling apart inside. It was interesting that I trusted a man rather than a woman with this aspect of myself – a fact of which I was aware but which I did not understand for many years.

I struggled on, with no respite from the awareness of growing darkness internally. My minister was about to move to another church, and before he did so met with me again. This time as he prayed with me I broke down, sobbing. It was as if I'd touched some part of myself that was out of my control and totally unknown. Although I knew where I was and who I was at that moment, some other terrifying and painful reality from the past was infinitely stronger. Eventually I calmed down enough to return home. At one level I almost felt cleansed by the tears and a sense of relief, but at another level I was in turmoil. What did it all mean? For as long as I could remember I was aware of something missing in my sense of who I was. I remembered almost nothing of my childhood, and seemed at times to be going through the motions of my life without really being there. I knew instinctively that the pain, terrifying as it was, seemed more real than much of my previous existence. But I did not want to look at where it came from or what it meant.

The minister left. I battled on in a state of bewilderment and wished I could try and make sense of the feelings of pain, which remained. Then I thought about Alistair's comment and decided I would write to let him know what had happened. Rationally I told myself he might be interested simply to know the end (as I thought of it) of a story in which he had played a part. Little was I to know it was to herald such a significant beginning.

I wrote to Alistair and told him how I had broken down. It was supposed to be a letter to say 'See, I'm fine now'. However,

I had grossly underestimated Alistair's ability to read between the lines – or, perhaps at an intuitive level I had written the letter specifically in the hope that he would read between the lines. I thought no more about it and was genuinely surprised when he arrived at work one day saying he thought I might like to talk. We found somewhere private and I talked about what had happened since I had met him last. It felt very strange. Until I had talked to my minister I had never talked to someone in that way about my life. Friends, yes, but not someone who would listen with that kind of attention. It also felt odd that Alistair said what time he would go – time boundaries was a counselling tradition I had never experienced. I expected him to pray and felt puzzled that he didn't – although also relieved. My experience of prayer had been that it raised in me volcanic emotions I had no wish to be in touch with – especially in the middle of a working day. At the end of the time Alistair asked if I would like to meet with him regularly to talk things through. I was genuinely astonished at the offer. I couldn't think why he would want to do that. I also had expected him to shore up my view that all was now well. I had got something out of my system and could go back to normal. A small part of me knew that wasn't true but I was not prepared to listen to it. Yet that small internal voice meant I did not dismiss his offer. I did take time to think about it, which says something about my lack of ability to ask for what I wanted and something, too, of my reluctance to begin this exploration. Given the rocky terrain we were to travel together the reluctance was perhaps appropriate. I contacted Alistair and the first official 'appointment' was fixed. The die was cast.

I don't suppose either of us knew at that time what a significant relationship this was to prove – certainly I didn't. I thought talking to him would fit neatly into my working day and soon I would be my old self again. I never dreamed that I would see him for three years and that it would serve not to preserve the old self but allow a very new self to emerge. I do remember that in one of the very first sessions Alistair asked me how I felt. I was completely unable to answer the question. I can still recall him describing to me his own feelings – beginning with feeling comfortable in the chair despite some backache – to attempt to give me some language to use and indeed some idea of what he meant. The world of feelings seemed entirely foreign to me.

For many of the early sessions we talked about my life thus far. I felt there was little to say. I had been brought up in a rural area of Wales, the youngest child of three – there were two older boys. In fact, I too had been a twin – though the similarity with Alistair's journey I did not know then. I had a twin sister who died shortly after birth. Only recently have I realised the long-term impact of the sense of living with someone else, the same and yet not the same, whom I never had the chance to know. It was as if I had to live her life as well as, or perhaps instead of my own.

What I had done, in fact, was to create for myself a fictional childhood to cover the fact that I could remember almost nothing of it. I told people the country setting was idyllic, my parents loving, and the only difficulty my father's death, which was dealt with. I only slowly began to realise, as Alistair listened to the story again and again, that this did not relate to the facts I knew. My brothers remembered my father as a harsh man who punished them for anything that was not 'manly'. My mother had told me that my father had been in a mental hospital although she had never said why except that he worked too hard. I began to realise that some of the family practices I thought were normal – for example that my father took me on holiday while my mother took my brothers, and the fact that my father almost always took me where he was going – even to work – while my mother stayed home – were in fact far from it. At these times I would wait – outside his workplace, or even outside the pub – in the car. To this day I dislike waiting for people in the passenger seat of the car.

Even though I had slowly begun to realise my rehearsed version of events did not fit the facts, I was still unprepared for what happened next. As the memories of my father's sexual abuse of me began to surface, I felt as though my whole world inside had exploded. The pain seemed unbearable. I felt as though I did not want to go on, either with the counselling, or indeed with living. Yet at another level I desperately needed the time in counselling as it was the one place I could be real. It was as if inside I was a raw, bleeding mess, yet I had to hide this at all costs. Another poem describes well the split I felt between my internal and external reality:

> She stood before the mirror.
> Pain-glazed eyes stared back
> Dull and lifeless
> Mirroring the soul within.
> Stroke by stroke the make-up is applied:
> Mask of deception skilfully covers.
> Morning is here: and so again
> The broken-hearted clown
> Faces her audience to give
> The finest of performances.

It is interesting that I even had to write this poem in the third person. The memories – although they made sense of so much which had puzzled me – meant I had to reassess myself and indeed my whole family totally, in particular my father. Initially, in reaction to my previous idealisation, there was a red-hot rage I was totally ill-equipped to deal with. Anger had never been permitted in my family, and my Christian faith had served to reinforce a view of anger as wrong and indeed as dangerous. I remember constantly expressing the wish to Alistair to go somewhere and be allowed to scream. The idea also frightened me, however, and was indicative of the fact I could not get angry in counselling, at least not very much. So the fantasy of somewhere to scream was also a way of avoiding my anger. Perhaps not surprisingly, I began to turn the anger against myself. However, whatever I tried did not work:

> No liquid anaesthetic
> Will dull the pain
> From every corner
> Of a broken spirit
> Whose silent cries
> Unheard for years
> Scream out from every cell.
>
> Yet pain,
> which seems to herald only death

> May yet prove birth pangs
> If this frightened, tiny child within
> Will, risking all,
> Reach out a hand to trust
> And find it grasped and held.

I can remember still Alistair's response when he read this poem. He said little (or I do not recall it) but simply held out his hand to me and for a moment held my hand. I felt at that moment deeply understood. Even thinking back now as I write this I have had to pause as there is a sense of standing on holy ground. At that moment he had seen the extent of the damage to this child who I still was and had been able to bear and indeed 'hold' it in this simple way. It was particularly striking as Alistair normally never touched me at all. This was in direct contrast to the church background I came from, where people tended to hug without asking and to touch frequently. Since I am a naturally tactile person – almost craving of physical affection – I at times felt this distance keenly but realise now it was vital. I needed to feel that someone knew how to keep clear boundaries and limits and to value me without my meeting any of their needs. At times I found the boundaries – especially the time one as often it took me so long to access my feelings that it was the time to end – very difficult but I can see how important it was in the healing process.

Perhaps it did not help in the process of revealing my inner world in counselling that all of my childhood had been spent in secrecy and silence:

> Pain
> Is not for public consumption.
> It should be kept
> Like secrets
> In darkness and silence.

This secrecy meant that I was a private person – still am, but in a very different way. Looking back, I realised very recently why it was I was able to be counselled about the abuse by a man. For many people who have been abused, only a woman could under-stand and they, not surprisingly, find men difficult to trust. I realise

that in a sense for me to be counselled by a man was the only
possibility. My experience had taught me that women could not
cope with emotion – my mother's life in care had left her out of
touch with the world of feelings in a profound way. The fact that
I had tried to talk to my mother about the abuse – albeit very
vaguely – and had been dismissed meant that at one level I
concluded that only a man would actually believe what I said.
The abuse was a secret my father and I shared and then became a
'secret' Alistair and I shared. The fact that Alistair's boundaries
were so clear prevented a collusive and destructive repetition of
my childhood patterns and meant that the parallels were reparative
not damaging. Another area where this sense of boundaries was
so vital, looking back, was in the handling of feelings. My
(unconscious) view was that there were two ways to deal with
feelings. Like my mother, they could be buried out of sight and
not felt at all. Or, like my father, they could be overwhelming
and destructive. As I began to access my feelings I frequently
feared, and dreamed about, breaking down completely. The regu-
larity of the counselling sessions and Alistair's calm acceptance of
my chaotic inner world prevented this from becoming reality. But
I think it was vital, too, that he was in fact in touch with his own
feelings. I was not often aware of them – not least because I was
too wrapped up in my own – but at times I was given a glance –
either because he chose to reveal them or because they slipped
through.

> We sit,
> Me with my unshed tears
> You with your knowledge and compassion.
> Sometimes we connect
> And tacitly you give me permission
> To be real.
> Today
> I sensed your tiredness
> And a bruising
> That comes from caring
> And receiving anger.
> So I was silent

> Afraid my silence
> Would cause you anger
> But more afraid
> My speaking would.

The rare occasions when Alistair revealed what he felt were almost always helpful, if always surprising. The one I recall most clearly came at the most desperate stage of my time in counselling. I had lost all hope of ever coming through the darkness I felt. One evening I gathered all my tablets, drank everything I could find in my bedsit and put the tablets out to swallow. I am still not sure why I didn't. Two days later I went to counselling and was hesitant to say anything about it. I thought Alistair might think I was attention seeking or trying to shock him in some way. In the end I did tell him. There was a short pause and I waited for the criticism. Quietly he said, 'I am really glad you didn't, Rachel.' I knew he meant it. By this time I had learned he would not say something he did not mean.

I suspect that this event and another different encounter with death were partially responsible for a turning-point in my descent into despair. A relative of mine died, and I went to see him in the chapel of rest. He had clearly gone – only his body was left. As I wrote at the time:

> Today I literally
> Stared death in the face.
> Gaunt and white
> With clenched left hand
> On purple satin.
> Stiff and cold
> Bearing no resemblance
> To him I knew.
> Today I decided
> I will choose life.

I was not aware of the subtle shift at the time, but it was there. There was still enormous amounts of work to be done. I struggled with understanding what my father had done. Seeing that he was ill did not either excuse him or indeed help. One of the things I found intensely painful was that his sexual needs had both been responsible for my creation and for my current pain:

> I am
> Half of you.
> Without your love-act
> I could not exist.
> Such irony then
> If that same love-act
> Which created me
> Carried within it
> In later years
> The seeds
> Of my destruction.

I needed to talk over this repeatedly. I certainly made progress, though there were aspects of the abuse, including the part my relationship with my mother, or lack of it, played which needed work years later in a second spell of therapy with someone different. There are aspects, too, which still cause me pain at times, but in a much more containable way than those three years. I sometimes think of my time with Alistair as rather like life-saving 'treatment' after trauma, and later counselling as reconstructive surgery. Both have been part of my whole life experience, all of which combined have led to my being the person I am now.

Not surprisingly, one of the areas I struggled with was the whole idea of fatherhood and intimacy. As well as profound personal implications, this affected my sense of my own faith. I had eagerly embraced fundamentalist Christianity as an adolescent – I think in retrospect as a search for a new and safe family where I could complete my growing up. However, in a sense that clear-cut faith served – for me – to stop my growth. When I felt at my most desperate, it seemed that the message of the Church was to have faith and praise God. This made me feel even more alienated – it seemed as though everyone else, in an image from the story of the Match Girl, was enjoying the feast while I was in the cold:

> You raised
> Your hands

In worship
And closed your eyes.
Worship concluded
You greet me
Eyes still closed
To all the pain.
Enquired after me
And I opened
My mouth to speak
But you continued
On your way.
I walked away
More lonely
Than I had come
And much more desperate
As again the match girl
Dies in the cold
Whilst looking wistfully
Through the window
At the feast.

Of course my depression meant I did not often share and give people the chance to prove me wrong. But my perception of the experiences of others was that the church found it hard to cope with long-standing difficulties. Perhaps they caused too much questioning and the pain of that was defended against by ignoring the problem or finding a simplistic solution. On one occasion I shared with a church leader how hard the last few months had been. He said he would pray and tell me what God said. He never mentioned the subject again. Did God have nothing to say to me? I felt keenly the loss of my previous comforting certainty:

Familiar tune
And – unexpectedly –
Pictures re-run in my memory.
Another life, another world.
Where did she go,
That girl who danced for You?
Who stole her away

And left this broken puppet
To live out a life
That promised much
And yields so very little?

I also began to realise how unhelpful some Christian terminology can be. I listened to one sermon on intimacy with God
with growing horror and when it was said that intimacy means
'to lean forward to kiss' I felt sick. Worse was to come when it
was said that God wanted to be inside us. I wanted a relationship
with God but one that was somehow non-invasive. Less difficult
but still significant was the general male bias. Sermons abounded
on mighty men of God but not women. Women rarely preached.
I needed good role models of both sexes, yet it has been largely
from two counsellors, not the Church, that this reshaping of my
ideas has come. I needed these doubts heard and knew they could
not be heard in the Church. In time my faith took on a new
form, less certain but in a way more important. Now it was not
about behaviour but about God accepting my inner world and
valuing it. I know that some schools of Christian counselling hold
that if our relationship with God is right other things will fall into
place and we will find wholeness. For me it was the reverse. My
relationship with God had been stunted by my experiences. It
needed human help (in the shape of a 'good enough' therapist) to
allow my image of God to be corrected. Yet this new form of my
faith – which for me feels more vital and alive – is even now not
always understood. It can be seen as a lack of faith or even of
moral certainty. I often hear prayers for God to banish doubt or
cynicism. Yet I have found my questioning keeps my dialogue
with God an active and real one. It saddens me that I am often
not free to share it for fear of criticism and misunderstanding.

As time went on my exploration of my feelings about my father
went through changes which in retrospect are distinct. From the
original idealisation I had a long stage of hatred, mingled with
self-hatred, and anger. I could see only the destructive aspects of
our relationship. As time – much time – went on I began to
integrate mixed aspects of our relationship. There had been
moments where he had taught me things, when our relationship

was not confused. This did not minimise the damage but acknowledged the grief too. On one occasion Alistair encouraged me to
'talk' to my father about all these mixed feelings. I wept. Then he
and I took some flowers to a local park and put them in a particular
place. To have someone share in both my anger and my love for
my father and keep both of those realities was vital.

When Alistair said he was leaving the area I had very mixed
feelings. I was aware I was much 'better' than I had been and
knew at one level that I would cope. I was equally aware though
of much that still needed working through. I was also by this time,
however, able to see Alistair as a separate person with his own
needs and life story. It helped me greatly that he communicated
to me that he knew ending would not be easy for me and that
there would be time to say what I felt. As so often, a poem
encapsulates what I came to feel:

> Harbours
> Are safe places.
> Storm-weary vessels
> Need their protection
> For small repairs
> Or – sometimes –
> A complete rebuilding.
>
> But ships
> Are built
> For open
> seas
> And, in time,
> Must lift anchor
> And set sail.

I felt when I said goodbye to Alistair that I would not see him
again. I was sad, but knew the 'rules' of counselling and accepted
them. I wrote from time to time to let him know how I was.
What I had not realised was that from this relationship was – over
the years – to develop a friendship which is one I cherish and
which enriches me. I am not too sure how it came about, except
that our paths came to cross professionally and to allow a more

adult-adult friendship to develop. It was something that happened rather than was intended. It might seem odd that a relationship of genuine equality can come from a relationship as unequal as the one we started with. Yet I think the seeds were sown then. As Alistair saw me at my worst, I, too, accepted him as he was – at times not understanding, or being distracted, or seeming to carry his own pain. These were things I was dimly aware of at the time but which did, I think, happen under the surface. I am aware as I write that it could seem as though my dependency was simply never worked through. However, I was to face those issues more in a second counselling relationship. The friendship we have now is not at all dependency based – I know how that feels! – but about a deep acceptance of each other as people, with similarities and differences. We value each other whilst recognising, indeed enjoying, our very distinct life journeys.

This account feels difficult to finish. I suppose that is because past, present and future are not always as distinct as we would like them to be. Part of the events I have described remain with me – especially as I have written this – yet in a way they are distant. The counselling relationship is past, yet the relationship remains in its new form. Both of us will have changed even by the time we read each other's accounts. So it is an account with an ongoing ending. Put simply though, both of us wrestling to become the people we are has, I believe, helped the other to do the same. God has used broken pieces of glass to recreate a colourful, ever-changing, stained glass window:

> We met
> When my pretty
> But unreal
> Stained-glass life
> Was shattered
> By unacknowledged shadows
> From the past.
>
> You stayed.
> Helped me face
> The sharp-edged fragments

I could not have borne
Alone.

You waited
As, together with the Master Artist
We re-created
A new
Infinitely more colourful
Vivacious life.

And I hope –
And believe –
That what you now see
Of this kaleidoscope life
Where joy and pain
Co-exist in ever-changing reality
Gives you a little joy.
And that, in moments of reflection
You too can see
The way the colours of my life are deepened
Because you are my friend.

Rachel.

8

INVESTIGATING THE
INSTITUTION

Air hissed, the padded metal bar descended, the slow motion of wheels turning vibrated with an awesome finality as the coach began to move. The height gave a panoramic view which twisted away in a sudden vortex of speed, wood and metal arcing to seeming destruction. The rollercoaster ride had begun. Having spent hour upon hour observing and facilitating groups in my experiential group therapy training, it was second nature to me to use these skills wherever I went. Even when I had no official role, I found myself being intuitively aware of the dynamics that were happening in groups in general and in institutions in particular.[1] My observations induced similar feelings to the terrifying yet exhilarating experience of a rollercoaster. The way groups work in institutions has the ability to be breathtakingly creative or savagely destructive. The institutions I have in mind are not churches, the dynamics of which I have already explored with their focus on two individual people in chapter 5; but rather theological colleges. I am bound to be influenced by the college I had most contact with. However, I have been a visiting lecturer in four theological institutions and have seen common patterns emerge. I have tried to form a composite picture involving elements of each because each presented me with the same basic dilemmas and questions. Why was so little attention paid to life together and the dynamics of the staff team? How was it that their relationships failed to demonstrate the Christian calling that was their *raison d'être*? It seemed to me that even a cursory knowledge of groups could have enabled these institutions to manage their lives in a more responsible, a more authentically human and ultimately Christian way. However, I only learned this knowledge the hard way after trying to introduce change into a theological institution.

With my arrival in a new church and having a role that freed me from some parish work, I took the opportunity to go and see the principal of a particular college, to discuss the possibility of running self-awareness groups, as part of their training programme. This concern arose out of my group therapy training after completing my own theological training. I wanted this to be not simply a sideline or 'somebody doing their own thing' but a real part of college life. My suggestion coincided with a report written by the director of a counselling service exploring patterns of training at a range of theological colleges. One conclusion this report highlighted was the lack of experiential groups within these colleges. The principal considered that these groups ought to be tried, despite, I gather, opposition from a number of faculty members, and so two groups began on an experimental basis, funded by the college. Attendance at such groups was open to any student in any year, on a voluntary basis. Their purpose was explained to the students as an exploration of the following: firstly, learning how to express our feelings, particularly what bothers us about ourselves or others; secondly, exploring how others experience us within the group; thirdly, discovering and learning to accept unknown or unacceptable parts of ourselves; and fourthly, experiencing affirmation within a group, whilst, at the same time, experiencing the adventure of growth and risk taking. Each term's sessions concluded with feedback from the group members about how much progress they felt the group, and they as individuals, had been able to make in these areas.

After the first year, the groups were continued and time was made available for the group facilitators to explain the role of self-awareness as part of ministerial formation at a preparatory weekend for new students. The college handbook now acknowledged the existence of the groups and gave an implicit recognition of their work, all of which was well received by the validating authorities. This was a positive achievement given the difficult climate that was around but such optimism was premature. During the third year of the groups' existence, the college faced a financial crisis and felt that it could no longer afford to support such groups. One group did continue on an expenses only basis for the facilitators, funded entirely by the students. What had happened was that these groups had been drawn into a broader, deeper, and as yet, underground or guerrilla warfare that had erupted in the college. The principal who had allowed this initiative to develop was asked to consider his future and this called into question the future of the groups. They did continue for another year but given the institutional momentum and no clear advocate in any position of power, they then ceased to exist. What lay behind this demise? How these groups were received can be explored by looking at the three parties involved, the staff, the students and the group facilitators.

Initially the staff were suspicious of these 'new' groups. One staff member questioned the ability of several of the facilitators to run such groups. Others raised questions about whether or not such groups would undermine their function of providing pastoral care and support for the students. It was somehow felt that a need for self-awareness groups indicated some failure on their part. It is not too difficult to see the real issues as being those of control, authority and the threat of something new which was beyond the experience of staff members. One could scarcely believe such attitudes as 'What do students need all this psychological nonsense for? What the Church needs is decent preachers'. All these factors were 'brought into the open' by the provision of self-awareness groups. Sadly, these issues were never directly dealt with in any face-to-face discussions between the group facilitators and the staff; rather they were expressed in the interaction (verbally and non verbally) in the staff room through the principal. If I, for example, made a comment as part of a general conversation, the riposte might be, 'That doesn't seem to be a very self-aware thing to say'. The whole issue of self-awareness was often treated with a jovial, 'let's have a laugh about it' attitude, which conveyed something of the discomfort around the issues involved. Yet what seemed to me to be a defensive use of humour, failed to acknowledge what the real issues actually were.

If someone is ambitious for power or control but not able to recognise this, that ambition does not go away. It goes underground and becomes part of our unconscious make-up. Here ambition can result in drivenness (an aspect I acknowledge in me) or a sensitivity to implied threat. Self-awareness groups, whilst a seemingly small part of college life, could be seen to be a threat, especially as they were supported by the principal. The significance of this will become clearer later in the chapter.

Those who attended the groups expressed a number of positive and negative views over the four years. Positively, the groups provided: a new style of group, different from anything else supplied by the college; a new pattern of leadership, which aimed to facilitate rather than taking the upfront leadership style modelled in the rest of the college; an emphasis on 'being' rather than formal didactic learning or doing set tasks; a place where it was safe to explore feeling which contrasted with the macho, male-leadership stereotyping that seemed to be generally approved of in both student and college structures; and a group where there was no assessment function and which was confidential in nature.[2] A few would go so far as to say that what they discovered in the group significantly changed their understanding of themselves and shaped their future ministry.

Negatively, some found the style of the group so different, and the anxiety this created so painful, that they retreated from real participation. This, however, provided the experience of how you hold and value in a group someone who is not always happy about being there; others found that the sessions, which took place outside the main lecture timetable, were simply too demanding after a busy day; and some were genuinely ambivalent as to the value of a self-awareness group.

Two of the original four group facilitators left, primarily because they questioned the value the college placed on the self-awareness groups and the college's unwillingness to examine the underlying issues in its training. Another left because his training with the Institute of Group Analysis clarified for him the realisation that the style and structure of the groups, in order to be acceptable for the college, would compromise their effectiveness. My own opinion was that, while I recognised the validity of my colleagues' views, to bring the groups to an end and cease any modelling of psychological issues related to ministry, would be to return to a deficient style of theological training.

The presence of self-awareness groups in a theological college unaccustomed to the style of such groups, raised issues for the institution, the lecturers and students. Little did I know when I proposed the setting up of self-awareness groups, how the next years would unfold. The tensions between the principal and staff steadily increased over this period and some of these tensions impinged on the groups. They had only started because of the support of the principal, but this very support made them suspect. I gained the impression that some felt they were 'just another of his new fads'. This was most clearly seen in the actions of one senior staff member who, while the principal was on sabbatical leave, suggested that in the light of the financial crisis of the college and the uncertainty around future staff appointments, the groups ought not to continue. There was no discussion with the facilitators, simply a letter in the post. I felt I had been neatly 'binned' like some disposable item past its sell-by date, under the guise of finance, when the real issues lay elsewhere.

Yet who were the forgotten people in this evolving power struggle? The students, who seemed to be peripheral to all that took place. While power and control issues were being encountered in the institution, they were also being encountered in the self-awareness groups. Here, however, it was from the perspective of how powerless they felt as part of the 'sausage machine'. The groups were in fact mirroring what was going on in the institution. As a group leader I did not feel heard by the staff, who in turn did not feel heard by the principal or the council and the students felt heard by none of these. It was a dialogue of the deaf, in desperate need to communicate with one another and yet not able to lip-read or sign. This further highlighted for me the question as to why the college existed. Was it really for the students? In the ensuing battle between the staff and the principal, the students, without whom the college could not exist, became mere bystanders, witnesses to some impending motorway pile-up. I don't know if this analysis is totally right but it seems to me that if vital issues are neglected or people pretend they are not happening or ignore them in the hope that nothing will happen, then there is a catastrophe in the making. More worryingly, what was being modelled in all this is that whoever has the power and is willing to use it, disguised in suitably Christian terminology such as 'it is for the good of the kingdom', wins. What an appalling prospect for future church leaders and how detrimental to the development of the Church as the dynamic, person-affirming community that I so want it to become.

The other dynamic experienced in the group was that of 'splitting'. Most of the groups had a male/female pair of facilitators who were variously seen as Mother/Father, Expert/Novice, Clergy/Lay person and so on. While I and the students were not aware of the extent of what was taking place between the staff and the principal, the self-awareness groups reflected 'splitting' as a major defence against anxiety. Putting it simply (as this is a complex area of psychodynamic theory) 'splitting' is a psychological mechanism learnt as infants as a way of coping with unmet needs. A mother cannot meet all a child's needs in the instant the baby experiences them. Therefore a baby learns to 'split' the life-giving mother (sometimes described as an 'object' in a more technical definition) into 'good' and 'bad'. If the mother meets his or her needs instantly she becomes 'good' but if these needs are not met then she becomes 'bad'. Over time babies cope with the fact that the mother, and they themselves, can be both 'good' and 'bad'. This enables them to cope with frustration, delayed desire and unmet needs. As adults we can still defend ourselves from threat or anxiety, especially when some need is not being met, by 'splitting' so that we become 'good' and they become 'bad'. In popular theological terms this can be seen in the way that some Christians ascribe all that is good to the work of God and all that is bad to the work of the Devil. The danger is that the 'bad' becomes anything we don't like, are afraid of, or does not meet our immediate need, and sometimes a 'demon' is held responsible for specific activity. This dualism surfaces in the Church from time to time, represented by such books as Peretti's *This Present Darkness*. I rather think that evil can still be found in me and that is where I need to wrestle, whilst still mindful of such biblical passages as Ephesians 6 which identifies the Christian struggle with 'principalities and powers'.[3]

Whilst all this was happening, group members also experienced a sense of belonging and of being held by the group, in which the painful process of trust was learnt again. This holding and containing is about facilitating people in a way that reveals their 'splitness' and allowing time for them to recognise both aspects of self and seeing how they can work together. Jungian writers refer to such ideas as persona and shadow. One application of this from a theological and spiritual perspective is found in Anne Townsend's book *Good Enough for God*.[4] It was in effect a holding environment I had provided for Rachel. Here the self-awareness groups were doing something similar, albeit in a much more limited way. For many of the group members this was a liberating experience which allowed the processes of self-awareness to take place. Perhaps in time the students may be able to model this to the institution (paradoxically, the students could teach their teachers) and I hope it was also something they were able to take into the Church.

The tensions partially uncovered in the running of the self-awareness groups were to be revealed, in all their grisly detail, like some post-mortem corpse, the following year. I was reminded of this episode in a scene from Susan Howatch's novel about the Church of England, *Absolute Truths*. Bishop Charles Ashworth writes about the problems he was having with his Dean.

> In the secular world potentially explosive procedures can be described in the language of power-politics and regarded as normal within a corporate structure; that is to say, the situation can be acknowledged without embarrassment and guilt. In the Church on the other hand, it is not 'the done thing' to talk of personality clashes and power struggles and boardroom battles. This does not mean that these unpleasant events never happen; it simply means that they are described in different language and dressed up in a variety of disguises . . . the secular world too is better equipped to deal with the fall-out of a corporate explosion; the chairman has the power to fire . . . and so although violence takes place in the form of sackings there is more scope for healing after the victims have gone. But I, as the Bishop, had no such powers . . . I could make recommendations in my report, but the Dean and

Chapter were not obliged to accept them . . . And how long would the shattered Cathedral community take to heal afterwards? There might be years of further division and strife.[5]

A very painful, complex and damaging situation had evolved at this college, that could easily grace the pages of any future Howatch novel. I subsequently learnt that the principal had been appointed by a governing body against the wishes of most of the staff members. This body thought they ran the college and the staff 'knew' they, the staff, ran the college. The new principal was caught in the middle, like some modern-day scapegoat. Under pressure and with little support, he may, in my opinion, have acted unwisely or not managed certain individuals well and this provided plenty of ammunition for those that chose to use it. The consequence was an ever-widening rift. Like some violent Western, the scene reached a climax with a shoot-out between a lone gunman and the cattle barons. This had no Clint Eastwood ending, where against all odds the lone gunman defeats all. The cattle barons won and the gunman left town, wounded but alive, to begin another life in another place. An exact blow by blow account of these events is not important and I could not tell it as I was only an interested outsider looking in. How and why had this come about? It seems to me there was a divergence between the council and the staff. The council had chosen a principal to introduce change and the staff would have preferred one of their colleagues for the post. If any existing staff member had been chosen, I think the college would have become like some dysfunctional family with everyone fulfilling their own allotted roles. Like keeping some family secret, such a family would act collusively to expel the outsider and this is a common enough dynamic that most institutions and companies have to wrestle with at some stage.

I came across similar dynamics as a member of a management committee of a voluntary mental health agency. We interviewed the project manager for a new, more senior post, and she was not successful. The anger within the organisation, where she was the popular choice, was considerable, yet in time most came to see that it was a more strategic and long-term view the committee had taken. Then she left for a similar post in another organisation, where she grew into the role with an authority she could never have had in her old post. In this case however the anger was addressed and dealt with before the new post holder arrived. On the other hand, in my view, the college staff were not able to deal with their anger; it was pushed underground, 'split-off' from its original source. What no one seemed to realise was that teaching students involves more than a cerebral transfer of information. A great deal of learning is unconscious, an intuitive 'picking-up' of messages, ideas or values; therefore this means that underground agendas become known at this unconscious level. If what is modelled is a deep unconscious split about unacceptable parts of self, how is that going to help any future church leader? What is vitally important is understanding the group dynamic processes that I saw at work here and which I have seen subsequently in other theological colleges. In my experience there appears to be a common problem in identifying unconscious processes but by their very nature they are hard to step back from, be aware of and work with, especially in training people for ministry. These unconscious forces often work against the stated aims of the institution and there is therefore all the more reason, for those within the institution to resist looking below the surface.

The predominant issues were power and control. These have been the fundamental issues at stake ever since the encounter of Adam and Eve, the archetypal man and woman who represent and speak for all other men and women, with the serpent, another archetypal being who represents all that is opposed to God. A knowledge of how institutions function from a psychodynamic perspective could have helped the institution understand the complex actions and reactions which occurred in the power struggle that developed between principal and faculty. In fact it was unnerving to see Bion's description and analysis of group activity fulfilled before my very eyes in textbook fashion.[6] Bion saw each group involving itself in two types of group activity: work-group activity focusing on the task that it had been formed to carry out; and basic assumption activity focusing on a variety of unconscious factors that come to life within it and obstruct the work-group activity. Groups are hugely complicated in their own right. Tom Douglas in his *Survival in Groups*, in a chapter on

'What goes on in groups', itemises fifty-eight processes. Yet when groups go wrong in the way they did at this college and in a way that the participants seemed to be unaware of, it seems to me that answers lie elsewhere, as in the area of Bion's basic assumptions. The task of the group was obscured by its drive to meet the unconscious needs of its members by reducing anxiety and internal conflicts. The irrational and chaotic behaviour seen in a group can be made clearer by seeing three factors at work: the need for dependency, the need for pairing and the need for fight or flight.

A theological college can become a defensive institution where there is a need in a staff team to be protected: from the competition of other theological colleges, from the demands of external validation, from the demands of churches as well as a denominational hierarchy and from the demands of a pluralistic and cultural relativism, to name but a few. The students have dependency needs, too, because they are in an unfamiliar and threatening environment facing demands to conform to standards and be assessed. It is likely they will look to the staff to meet their needs. If the staff are uncomfortable or unskilled, this can be experienced as another threat which they in turn look to a leader to protect them from. When also faced with the internal demands of students wanting to push new boundaries – some no doubt working through unresolved adolescent issues – as well as a governing body not quite in synchronisation with all that was going on, then it is understandable that dependency issues are raised for the staff. One theological factor that might have further obscured this need for dependency is the assumption that all needs are met by God and it is therefore unnecessary for us to have these needs met by groups or others. A group dominated by an unconscious need for dependency looks to a leader who will look after, protect and care for the members of the group and make them feel good and feel safe, especially from outside forces.

I would argue that it is psychodynamically healthy to acknowledge one's dependence and work towards interdependence. If the staff team in any institution were to fail to recognise their dependence on the governing body, then rivalry rather than interdependence could be the result. Such a rivalry is the very antithesis of the Christian faith. If a competitive situation emerges, the leader can sustain the group who believe him to be all-powerful and all-knowing and who avoids changing the organisation because of the anxiety this situation raises for the group. The former principal, as a warm caring father-figure, fulfilled this idealised role. Idealisation is another defence mechanism whereby someone is elevated or overvalued in the mind of another person in a way that does not accord with reality. Someone can become the perfect father or mother, where we choose to ignore or are unable to see their faults and failings. It seems to me the staff team had been led by an indulgent parent, unwilling to 'rock the boat' where the 'children' were able to do what they wanted, without much real accountability. This is an additional danger that I think is encountered when staff members have formerly been church leaders, where it was entirely possible for them to do much as they wished without referring or being answerable to anyone. This underlying attitude is then brought into college life. With such a principal, the idealisation continues once they have gone. So as the college was looking for a new principal, no one could possibly have been 'good enough'. The governing body made their assessment and interviewed three candidates, nominating the person whom they considered best for the college. They reached this conclusion, I understand, from their perspective which was that the college needed a general 'shake-up'. The staff team did not share this view, took one look at their new principal and reacted in what seems to me a cavalier fashion. The scene was set for the former principal to be further idealised and the new principal castigated. The group when faced with 'his fallibility, or when evidence of this becomes too great to be ignored',[7] disposed of him abruptly. Before this happens two other forces are often at work.

While this unconscious dependency is reverberating around, it leads to a desire to look for help either from within or without. A 'new' potential leader is identified within the group, new pairings emerge as the group dissolves into a shifting complex of alliances. Yet this potential leader never can become the leader because this phase is still one of idealisation. This person's strengths become magnified and his or her faults and limitations are ignored. If he or she also harbours a secret desire for the coveted role, the dynamics are explosive. The explosion is caused by the tension generated between overt structures, that deal with the acknowledged agendas, and covert structures that deal with the unconscious agendas. The friction of these two structures grinding against each other may cause a spark to ignite in an inflammable situation. The other alternative is one of implosion when the weight of the overt structures cannot withstand the weight imposed on it by the covert structures. While all this is happening,

> Group members lose their critical faculties and individual abilities, and the group as a whole has the appearance of some ill-defined but passionately involving mission. Apparently trivial matters are discussed as if they were matters of life and death, which is how they may well feel to the members of the group, since the underlying anxieties are about psychological survival . . . the group closes itself off from the outside world . . . A questioning attitude is impossible; any who dare to do so are regarded as foolish, mad or heretical . . . Effective work, which involves tolerating frustration, facing reality, recognizing differences among group members and learning from experience is seriously impeded.[8]

The scene is set then like some blood-soaked act from *Macbeth*. The dynamics outlined by Bion suggest that there is a uniting against an internal 'enemy' that needs to be expelled from the group as quickly as possible, in order for the group to survive and for anxiety to be reduced. 'People, ideas and institutions so identified are mercilessly divested of power and demolished.'[9] As the extent of the issues became clear to the governing body, the students and the wider Church community, some reconciliation was attempted, but this failed, in my opinion, because the unconscious agendas and covert structures were not recognised. It was a time of great disillusionment and hurt. It was a poor advert for the Christian faith, with its emphasis on forgiveness. It was heart-rending to listen to the pain of the principal, who went on 'indefinite sabbatical leave' at the point of emotional breakdown, as he recalled events and emotions (admittedly from his perspective) that had tragedy etched all over them.

Yet there is another way of interpreting these events, which parallels and further illuminates this psychological perspective. One can reflect theologically on these events as a way of understanding what can happen in theological colleges or other institutions such as the Church. Issues of power and control take me back to the biblical narrative found in the early chapters of Genesis. Into this saga of bewildering creativity, tender sexuality, mystery and majesty, and authentic and complementary relationship, comes a shattering that fragments and distorts all these good things like a knife slashed across a great work of art – as indeed happened to Salvador Dali's haunting and ethereal *St John of the Cross*. This shattering is the fall of Adam and Eve, tempted by the serpent – a symbol that there is both a being and a power of evil in the world that is utterly opposed to God.[10] Yet 'If Satan is present in the story of Genesis 3, he is wearing a careful mask. He is hidden in the ordinariness and everydayness of a creature in the Garden.'[11] Adam and Eve sought power and control and they speak for all of us. This ancient myth[12] speaks truthfully and powerfully to us today like a booming voice through a megaphone. There is something in everyone that desires these things. I find in the 'fall' with this all-consuming desire for power, subtle references to the basic drives or instincts of human nature, sexuality and death, both described and built into a psychological framework by Freud. While some see this as a far too mechanistic understanding of human nature, Freud himself saw the mythic quality of his discoveries.[13] Another psychoanalyst, Bettelheim describes life this way,

> For Freud, the I was a sphere of tragic conflict. From the moment we are born to the moment we die, Eros and Thanatos struggle for dominance in shaping our lives, and make it difficult for us to be at peace with ourselves . . . It is this struggle which makes emotional richness possible; . . . which gives life its deepest meaning.[14]

These psychological references help my theological reflection because they remind me that the text of this Genesis event cannot be closed off like closing a book. They resonate in us here and now. It is easy and glib to make a theological principle out of this 'fall', it is more difficult to recognise the extent of the fallenness

110

in us. This same desire for power and control is in us and was in this situation of conflict at the college. The hurt and duplicity that I observed would have had the enemies of God shouting in triumph. What seemed to me to be at work was the re-living of this Genesis saga. One theologian has described the fall as permeated with the 'hermeneutic of suspicion'[15] which leads to 'sin . . . complex, involved, multivalent, like an octopus with its spreading tentacles or like a cancer with its manifold metastases.'[16] The ordinariness and everydayness of college life where every event, action, and comment were regarded suspiciously made it an awful place, if one just looked below the surface. There could only be one outcome once events had become as distorted as this but the cost was immense and it seemed to me to be borne more by a sacrificial scapegoat than by any other. This experience suggests that the issues of power and control, shown to be powerfully at work in the lives of individuals and an institution, are to be ignored at one's peril. The tragedy seems to me to be that given some psychological understanding and a greater ability to wrestle with the actual experience of a theological and spiritual dimension to life, there could have been a far less damaging outcome.

What other possible scenarios could be envisaged? What could have made a difference? The staff group could have been facilitated by an external person as a way of unearthing the real agendas that are always around but often remain hidden (this is true for any organisation, but Christian groups find such issues more difficult to acknowledge). This is one way of defusing the destructive forces that we so often push into some underground bunker, in the hope that we will be safe from them. While this suggestion was made to the principal before some of the troubles became apparent, he recognised that it would not be acceptable to the staff. A second option could have been the development of a system of appraisal, so that individual staff members could see how they performed in an objective way. This idea always seems to be initially rather frightening but it can clarify and give fresh perspective on one's work, especially when it gives due recognition for work done well. An individual sense of worth enables a greater sense of interdependence and reduces the need to be dependent

111

on the valuing of or belonging to a group. Another option could have been an acknowledgement and a working with the more negative aspects of self that made their appearance. This would probably have required some personal therapy or spiritual direction. These options may have brought about the recognition that one can so easily make an idol of hurt and grievance. In this painful conflict, a whole range of people, including the neglected and powerless students, were hurt. Such is the allure of hurt and grievance (an enticing and addictive brew of which I have drunk), that it easily becomes an idol and makes forgiveness difficult. Such painful memories can become a fertile breeding ground for any sin to become deadly as the spiritual being of a person becomes poisoned. Yet it is in our very woundedness, where we are forced to face our vulnerability and the bleaker aspects of self which we 'split off', that God longs to work in bringing shalom – a wholeness of being.

A second theological reflection is (and this is a difficult issue for some Christians and institutions to recognise) the existence and pervasive influence of the unconscious. Why events happened the way they did was because this aspect of life had not been taken into account. Some theologians, such as Theissen, recognise Christianity as a confrontation with the unconscious and use this approach to explore aspects of Paul's psychology.[17] Just as unconscious processes can be seen to be at work in individuals, they can also be seen to be at work in institutions. So when a playgroup using church premises complains about not having enough cupboard space, they may also be saying unconsciously, 'We are not given enough space or recognition within the life of the church.' As this situation has recently occurred in my current church, I recognise that both the conscious and unconscious needs are a genuine expression of the real situation. Yet churches and Christian institutions fail to recognise that God is transcendent and beyond us, immanent and near us, inside and outside us, at work with our whole being – body, mind and spirit, consciously and unconsciously, equipping through natural intuition and spiritual gifting – in order to make us whole and bring wholeness to others. For an institution which claims to work for the glory and honour of God to fail to recognise the diversity, breadth and scope of his being and ways of working in us, is to come close to dishonouring him.

A third theological reflection is that institutions find the pain and challenge of change remarkably difficult to handle. A clear demonstration of this was seen in a fascinating television series written by the former ICI business guru, John Harvey Jones. In each programme he acted as a consultant to various-sized British companies with the aim of helping them become more efficient. At times he was at the point of despair as not only did the existing management fail to see the problem (which was immediately apparent to him) but even when they did see, they failed to implement the suggested changes because they were too painful. His conclusion was that for British industry to survive into the twenty-first century it would need to learn to react quickly and flexibly to changing needs and demands, something that some companies would not do. Theological colleges need to embrace a willingness to change if they are to survive into the twenty-first century and carry on training people to lead churches in a creative, life-affirming way. Yet so often they fail to do so because it is a painful struggle. Halton addresses this same issue, the avoidance of pain.

> Like individuals, institutions develop defences against difficult emotions which are too threatening or too painful to acknowledge ... They may arise from internal conflict between management and employees ... some institutional defences, like individual defences, can obstruct contact with reality and in this way damage the staff and hinder the organization in fulfilling its task ... Central among these defences is denial [and] ... Resistance, that is, an emotionally charged refusal to accept or even to hear what [is said].[18]

This avoidance of pain (individually or institutionally) is deeply ingrained in us in physiological as well as psychological pain. In one of the classic discussions on suffering, C.S. Lewis makes the point that pain is not of itself a bad or negative experience.[19] Similarly Christian institutions also need to heed this point. Pain, threat and anxiety in an institution need to be faced in order not to be frozen or stuck in some ongoing dynamic that defends itself well but fails to meet the needs – the real needs – of those within as well as those without. This is particularly true for institutions which exist to train others to lead institutions, namely churches. What is modelled is an avoidance of pain, a strengthening of defences[20] and a failure to engage with the whole nature of people, their good and their bad, their persona and their shadow.[21] It is fairly easy to see these patterns being repeated in churches. Churches want a theology of success, not of failure because failure is too painful to bear. We can all learn from Winnicott that in the end we succeed by failing but failing the clients' way.[22] The Church exists for the benefit of those not yet in it and paradoxically we defend ourselves in so many ways from really engaging with people, at whatever stage of spiritual and psychological health.

As I now reflect on this time as a psychoanalytically informed observer, I realise that I had taken up a 'listening position on the boundary between conscious and unconscious meanings' where I began to 'make sense of these hidden references to issues of which the group itself was not aware.'[23] Yet it also made me question the whole place of theology, and realise that I was still unaware of much that was within myself. What I could see in others, I was not sure I could see so clearly in myself. It was this that made me decide to go into personal therapy.

9

THE JOURNEY WITHIN

I knocked at the door. I felt sick, anxiety gripped my stomach, as my mind raced through scenario after scenario. What would he be like? What was I going to say? Tony opened the door and welcomed me in. I cannot remember much more other than his opening words 'Tell me a bit about yourself?' Hobson, an eclectic psychodynamically influenced psychotherapist, suggests the first five minutes of therapy are crucial.

> A very great deal can happen within a very few minutes. Great revelations are rare, and even profound insights can never be fully lived out in a long lifetime. Yet a step, just a little step, forward can be an important movement in growth; it can open up a new path to explore. . .[1]
>
> It is . . . difficult, frightening, and hazardous to commit myself to a personal relationship in which, in an unknown way, I shall be changed.[2]

That little step seemed like standing at the top of a sheer cliff face, the wind roaring, a hang-glider strapped to my back, and an inner voice saying 'jump'. How long would it take for the fear and panic to turn into exhilaration? Would I plummet downwards like some earth-bound meteorite, to embed myself in the ground? What Tony did, in allowing me 'space' to be me, dealing with issues to do with separation from internal parents, twin, siblings and church, he did well. In fact, I would go as far as to say that the seeds of this book were sown in my thinking and etched on my emotions in therapy as I worked through the convoluted twists and turns my life had taken. What I thought were straight and smooth pathways, like ancient Roman roads, were in fact cobbled, rutted and pot-holed. The next eighteen months raced by. I learnt to trust myself and my intuition as I came to see that Tony trusted me. I came to see that the defence I most often used was my academic grasp of something. I had never thought of myself as an intellectual but a close friend once told me that she found me 'chilling' when she saw me switch into this mode. She felt as if she was seeing a different me, no smile, no warmth, a clinical more remote being. I also came to see that my second most commonly used defence was my evangelical faith.[3] It was and is a very real part of me but I was challenged by Tony to see beyond it and to engage in a real intimacy with God, to see beyond the Bible and encounter Christ, the Word of God, that my 'brand' of faith was protecting me from. I still find a close relationship with God – for myself – something elusive and complex that I never quite seem to manage. Paradoxically I experience an intimacy and a distance from God at the same time, which I shall explore in the next chapter. I can be that person of faith for others, but I feel I have barely started for myself. I learnt to be honest with myself and offer that honesty to others in a way that some perceive as disarming and engaging and others perceive as arrogant and a threat. In Tony I found someone who was as honest with me as I felt I was with others. Perhaps what I benefited from most however was his sense of pace and timing.

> To be understood is reassuring but to be penetrated by means of someone else's mysterious knowledge of my 'inside', with the danger of possession and damage, is a threat to my identity. In 'togetherness', contact is experienced as a meeting in a 'space-between' . . .To enter into a mutual conversation is an act of faith, a leap in the dark, which is very different from a tenacious clinging to a belief.[4]

Tony nurtured a real Alistair into being, a less dependent, more risk-taking, less split-off person. All this came about through a relationship. Like all important relationships it required risk in order to develop into something significant. As I talked and Tony listened, he was willing to express comments on my theology as well as my psyche. This therapeutic relationship helped me discover the ability to question more and face up to various external and internal authority figures. I reflect with amusement that it took me a year to have enough courage to ask what his therapeutic qualifications were, as I had gone to him trusting the recommendation of a colleague. I experienced a real sense of trust in Tony but it still took me a year to believe at an emotional, as well as at an intellectual level, that I was 'good enough'. This relationship enabled me to be more risk-taking in my theology, as at its heart there was a real relationship that went far beyond my previous understanding of God. Winnicott talks about a real or true self and a false self, where the false self protects us and is shaped by what we want others to see. Slowly, and it is a process that is still going on, my true self emerged but now as my true self what do I think and believe about God and how does this fit with the crucial dimension of relationship?

In my experience of darkness, and that glimpse of the abyss, that I encountered with Rachel and which I saw at work in the Church and theological institutions, I discovered personally how easy it is to live a split, dual existence, where there is a real collusion between the two differing aspects of self. It is my own experience that has given me particular insight into seeing this in others, and especially in the Church. As I look back on my journey of faith, I had encountered God in a conversion experience and so begun a Christian life; been influenced by other Christians; acquired an intellectual knowledge by reading and reflecting on Scripture; learnt a theological language to help me try to understand and describe God; and heard a real 'call' to work in the Church. As I have moved on in this journey, as more truly me, my knowledge, experience and 'call' have grown with me. I know with less certainty, I experience a living tension as I balance what I believe and the way I behave; and have seen my call become more specific, in terms of helping and holding people in the damaged and hurting areas of their lives. This has made me reflect again and again on my theology and has helped me experience it as well as think it.

One of the major consequences of this time in therapy and wrestling with the relationship between theology, psychiatry and psychoanalysis for a research degree was the start of a search for a psychodynamic theology. The search, like that for the Loch Ness monster, proved fruitless yet still left me with the sense that it was out there somewhere. Surely if I explored the almost fathomless depths of theology that go beyond my understanding, some dynamic theology could be found. I came to see that if I were to discover anything, the place to begin was in fathomless depths of my own being and my hungry intellect. Why was this search so important? For me this stage in my spiritual and psychological journey was one of integration, of uncovering the 'splits' in me and moving towards resolution. I see this as a desperate need within Christians, the Church, theological institutions, indeed, in contemporary culture as a whole. Why else has counselling and psychotherapy become not only popular (popular tastes can change) but so necessary? I began to work on a psychodynamically informed theology as a way of reconciling two radically divergent disciplines that had much that could enrich each other. Part of my aim in writing this book is to offer theological and therapeutic insights that have proved illuminating for me and that I hope will shed light on others' stories. There are huge dangers in this venture as other 'boundary-dwellers' have discovered in entering this 'no-man's' land, uncertain which side will shoot first. Writers working from psychological and theological perspectives have described this 'no-person's' land. Brian Thorne explores the tension of living at the boundaries of psychology, whilst Hannah Ward and Jennifer Wild describe what it is, theologically, to be a 'boundary-dweller'.

> A boundary separating inside from outside is no fine line, but resembles a gap that must be traversed with care . . . that is full of creative potential as well as threatened disintegration and breakdown. Those who find themselves on or near the boundary – those we call 'boundary-dwellers' – are not necessarily 'marginal' but rather on the threshold . . . of something new . . . In the experiences of many contemporary Christians there is a real sense of wilderness, a sense of having grown out of, or away from, old belief systems . . . We experience the present as barren and bewildering . . . but the new is beyond our grasp. How do those of us who dwell

uneasily on the boundaries . . . live there creatively, both for ourselves and for the wider Christian community?[5]

What I began to explore were four boundaries within which theological, spiritual, psychological and psychodynamic ideas could meet and encounter one another. These four boundaries are not like the ropes of a boxing ring, there in order to keep the occupants fighting. They are rather the four edges of a sketch map within which some incredible country can be traversed and some unknown treasure discovered. During this time my view of God evolved and moved away from the monolithic, rigid evangelical view I had before which I had seen reduce faith to a transaction rather than a living relationship.[6] The longer I remain a Christian, the more profound, mysterious, and complex God seems to become and as a consequence my view of God has also changed. This exciting phase of my life is the opportunity for an ever-changing, growing, dynamic theology, shaped in part by the people I have encountered and the experiences I have gone through. It is as much discovering new aspects and dimensions of a traditional faith affirmed as the historic faith – as found in Oden's systematic theology[7] – as it is in exploring new ideas that emerge from a variety of theological and psychological traditions. Yet this brings with it the fear or anxiety that it will provoke censure from those of an evangelical tradition that I still wish to be part of and feel 'rooted' in. I do, and in fact need, to belong – yet I also want to be apart. I want to be distinctive. I want to be me. The theological understanding I offer here is not original, though a part of me wishes it was. I am a thinker of others' thoughts; what may be new is the way I have put various aspects or themes together, in a way that illuminates God for people in their journey of struggle and pain. Other theologians may have provided the Lego bricks but I'm building my own structure, precarious as it feels at times. This endeavour has been helped by the discovery that a vital creative part of me is able to hold things in tension, to live with open-ended questions and an acceptance that I cannot supply all or even some of the answers.

What is the purpose of this psychodynamic theology? It is a theology from below, beginning from where people are, encountered in their spiritual and therapeutic need. It could also be described as a theology of trauma, dwelling with those traumatic aspects of life that conventional theology often overlooks. It really is a theology with a cross at its heart, not so much in an all-too-neat understanding of the atonement but in the entering into the depths of human pain and sin in order to restore relationship.[8] It is a psychodynamic theology because it gives due attention to the presence of the unconscious and takes seriously the truth content of psychodynamic insight. My theology may well be unique to me, but it has helped me and therefore I hope it will be a means of helping people truly to engage with themselves and with God. It is an interpretative framework that is solid enough to support the work I do and open-ended enough to allow others genuinely to meet me and, I hope, God. It is a structure built on good foundations, that are living, growing and changeable, yet also deep, immovable, and anchored in a relational God.

Let me dive then into this ocean (or should it be loch) of theological and psychodynamic insights and see what we can discover under the surface. In order to chart where we are diving, here is a simple map. There are four edges to this map showing the area of our sub-aqua explorations. Firstly, God is persons in communion (the triune God) and is therefore the source and end of all authentic relationships. Secondly, we encounter God in the story of God found objectively in Scripture and relationally in our lives and the lives of others. This narrative theology has a paradoxical dimension to it. Thirdly, God is paradoxical (hence the reason why narrative theology can be paradoxical) and we can and cannot understand who he is. We must therefore live with this tension, this paradox of the revelation and hiddenness of God. Fourthly, we can know something of God metaphorically, and the metaphors most accessible to people today are relational. This relational dimension takes us back into the triune presence of God. There is then a linking and an active, life-giving flow to this theological understanding, similar to that found in Lake's 'dynamic cycle' of being.[9]

These four linked themes are simply a rough sketch map that takes us to the buried treasure that I referred to at the end of chapter 2. It is not a detailed, contour by contour Ordnance Survey map. This is where I react against an evangelical subculture which portrays the Christian life in such a way. Even this sketch map would require a volume in its own right. I am content with the sketch map – so let me show two of its aspects in this chapter and another two in the next, in the hope that others will discover treasure for themselves, that ultimate treasure being the living God.

The map's north side points us to the concept and description of God as persons in communion. What do I mean? This is a helpful way of describing the doctrine of the Trinity. This priceless, unique, foundation of Christian theology has intrigued and astonished many major theologians down through the centuries. God, the origin of all things, the creator of all being, the source of all love, is one and three persons, Father, Son and Spirit (spoken of in personal terms in Scripture). God can be described and experienced as a community of persons. They 'are neither simply modes of relation nor absolutely discrete and independent individuals, but Persons in relation and Persons only through relation. Persons exist only as they exist for others . . . Persons are what they are only through relations with others.'[10] Luc Besson, the French film director, picks up this theme in discussing his film, *Leon*. He explores the similarities of the two central characters, a twelve-year-old adolescent girl, Matilda, and a middle-aged hit man, Leon. Both are alone in a corrupt and violent world. One is innocent, one is not. 'They are so different and they are the same . . . they need the same thing, some love and attention and they are lost . . . Leon is dead like a plant, a vegetable and then the door opens, the light comes in, life comes in, it's the girl.' Their ability to relate to one another enables them to become more authentic persons. God is like that. This also means that if God is denied, as much of contemporary culture denies him, 'The result is a defective . . . relationality, so that the central dimensions of our created being are ignored, suppressed or distorted.'[11]

The Christian faith speaks of an encounter with God, in which we are drawn by the Spirit through the Son to the Father. In this encounter we discover that 'God is not isolated singularity but communion and mutual self-giving. At the heart of all things there is a loving personal relational reality from whom life and love overflow for all.'[12] From this understanding of God we can see the huge importance of people and their relationships as we reflect God's creative and rescuing work in us. God, as persons in relationship, is then the source of all authentic relationship. Another theologian, von Balthasar (writing at a time when people were less aware of gender issues and who uses 'man' to mean both genders), continues this theme.

> Only when God is a person is man taken seriously as a person. The personhood of God, the cross of Christ, the dignity of man, and human life are indissolubly inter-related. One may imagine that one could advocate the dignity of man without believing in God's person, indeed precisely by denying it . . . Only the personal God himself whose love is truth and whose truth is love can give to the I and thou between men a truly personal quality, so that in the exchange in trust between the two something unique, something irreducible occurs . . . pure truth.[13]

That bond of trust forges a powerful relationship between Matilda and Leon, yet they, without God, are not yet capable of expressing that truth-bearing potential they contain. Such experience of personhood is not confined to Christian experience. That sense of trust described by von Balthasar is a crucially important psychological concept, to be explored in chapter 10.

The very best our relationships can offer is a flickering candle in response to the blazing searchlight of God, but when we are in darkness every lux of light is crucial to show us where we are and to move us on to his incandescent presence. The reason why I remain a Christian is my conviction that despite the great potential contained in people's lives and relationships (some realised, some not) they are simply the sparkler at a fireworks display, when they could be sharing in the radiance of the Creator God's sun. God is Person in relationship and all human relationships with their potential for creativity, love, affection, trust, risk and hope are but pale reflections of what God calls us to be in and through a relationship with him. This is what makes my faith evangelical still. I have a passionate commitment to bringing people into authentic relationship with God and to seeing this being worked out in their lives, no matter how damaged they have become.

People are relationship seeking. Bowlby, the pioneering child psychoanalyst writes,

> Intimate attachments to other human beings are the hub around which a person's life revolves, not only when he is an infant or a toddler or a schoolchild but throughout his adolescence and his years of maturity as well, and on to old age. From these intimate attachments a person draws his strength and enjoyment of life, and through what he contributes, he gives strength and enjoyment to others.[14]

We exist as we relate to other human beings. This seems so simple, yet is utterly profound and it explains why those haunting images of children left abandoned in their cots from the earliest age in Romanian orphanages were so chilling. Deprived of all but minimal human contact, unable to do more than whimper in a forlorn, now muted cry for help or stare with dark and dead eyes, what have they become? No doubt, hugely damaged individuals, who I hope might yet find some repair. People cannot exist on their own. We seek relationship intuitively because (from a theological perspective) we see this is how we were made to be and this is the authentic and attractive promise of faith. It is not a slavish adherence to rules and regulations, set by some tyrannical authority figure, such as I experienced in that small, Dickensian Scottish school, but to the One, the Lord, who is the source of all being and love. Persons are 'unfinished this side of heaven . . . If the fundamental thing to understand about persons from a theological perspective is that human beings are essentially persons in relation, then personhood is a process of becoming. The process is one of restoring the image, of growing into wholeness . . . of growing into full humanity. "We are persons on the way".'[15] This raises the questions of how we become and how we relate. These are some of the philosophical and theological questions raised by Freud's use of motivational drives and the structures of the mind. Different answers to these questions have given rise to different 'schools' of psychodynamic thought which have different emphases, but a common basic theory.[16] The most important difference is the move away from the rather mechanistic notion of 'drives' to the primacy of interpersonal relationships, especially the earliest ones, found in the work of Klein, Fairbairn, Guntrip, Winnicott and Kohut.[17]

To understand how we relate, Freud created a theory of psycho sexual development in which people work through distinct phases. These relate to the dependency of being fed, the independence of controlling one's desires and body (often focused on toilet training) and a sense of interdependence as one relates to a mother and father – separately and together. This is not the only psycho-logical theory explaining relationships but it is the one I use and makes real sense of the experience of the people I have seen. Each phase must be successfully passed through in order to produce a fully developed person. These are such significant stages of development that the failure of 'good enough' caring or 'good enough' transitions will inevitably have a major impact in adult development.[18]

Freud's metaphorical model of the mind introduced the con-cepts of the id, the ego and the super-ego to the internal dynamics of each person.[19] Put simplistically, the id is an unconscious aspect of personality that seeks pleasure and satisfaction above all else.[20] Every mother can tell of the immediacy of demand made by a hungry newborn baby wanting a breast. The ego is an aspect of personality that balances the demands of the inner world with the reality and demands of an external world. A baby discovers that demands which were met immediately when they were newborn, are not responded to in the same way now they are aged two. The super-ego is the source of moral and behavioural prohibitions based on internalised parental voices such as: 'Don't you dare do that again', 'How many times have I told you', and so on. A person generally learns to balance these competing aspects of being. However, imbalances do occur and may be evidenced in adult behaviour and feelings. If a client responds to a counsellor as an authority figure, there may be issues to do with an overly developed super-ego. There are dangers with such a simplification of these concepts – Freud recognised that people could take these ideas too literally,[21] Jacobs suggests that they are best understood metaphorically,[22] and Brown and Pedder acknowledge the inability of such theory to account for 'more complex interpersonal phenomena'.[23]

Our ability to relate to God is influenced (though not determined) by our ability to relate to others, especially our key parental figures with whom we form a triangular relationship. We develop a distinct identity with both our mother and father, they are not interchangeable for each other as generic parents. God is persons in communion in triangular relationship and our view of God is blurred or sharpened by this initial relationship. I went to buy a pair of binoculars and after I had tried several pairs, the salesperson offered me another. Looking through them I saw images of startling sharpness, clarity and dimensionality. When I commented on this the person smiled and said, 'They are made by Leitz and cost several hundred pounds', so I put them down as this was way beyond my price bracket. Our relationships blur our view of God, but when we encounter God directly (he is not beyond our budget) our vision of ourselves and others can be significantly enhanced.

This theory comes into its own in a therapeutic relationship. The therapeutic process facilitates the discovery of some aspects of these early stages which can be repaired or remodelled through a new relationship – which makes connection between the past and the present. Over the years a number of clients have come to see me because they are concerned about being single and find it difficult to make friends. In one case my supervisor has suggested (using this psychodynamic framework) that Sue could be stuck at a stage where she has a vital need to control and retain. Her gift of herself cannot be given to others because she is using all her resources to keep herself in check and she feels overwhelmed and threatened when others approach in some kind of relationships. As Sue has chosen to enter into counselling it may be the start of a relationship that allows her the space and time to risk 'letting go' without being rejected or punished as she may previously have been. Sue may begin to discover that not all authority figures that the counsellor can become, wish to reject or punish her or like her only if she is good. This happens through the presence of transference and counter-transference. Transference describes the process where a person repeats childlike patterns (at whatever stage they have become stuck or have been most significant) with their counsellor. It is a universal phenomenon, occurring in all relationships. What is distinctive about psychodynamic counselling is the use that is made of transference (and its counterpart in the therapist – counter-transference) as part of the therapeutic relationship. This can be positive – good thoughts, feelings or actions towards the counsellor – and negative – bad thoughts, feelings or actions towards the counsellor. At times the person will resist the dynamics occurring in the relationship and resistance needs to be overcome in a way that is creative for the person. Such a therapeutic relationship needs clear boundaries to help the person feel secure enough to risk a whole variety of feelings and memories which come to the surface. The north side of our psychodynamic theology (a more user-friendly term than 'a psychodynamically influenced theology'), represented in terms of a sketch map, is focused on relationship. God as persons in relationship can be experienced in our creation (the image of God in us), our redemption (a relationship of being made alive by faith) and our destiny (a relationship that transcends time and physical embodiment). These, however, find their original expression in the significant relationships of our lives. The relationality of God and the relationships offered by parents or care-givers resonate together and form a creative partnership, which like two ice-dancers skate in creative, skilful, awe-inspiring synchronisation.

The south side of this sketch map is formed by the very story, the words, images and textures of these relationships. There is a narrative dimension to faith which forms another boundary to this relational psychodynamic theology. In this God speaks and he does so by means of story, the story of God found in the Bible beginning in Genesis and ending (at least temporarily) in Revelation. We see the story of God unfolding step by step with mounting tension until it reaches its climax in Christ, the Word of God. However, God's making known of his personhood to us needs to have an objective form if it is not to fall into the trap of ultra-subjectivism.[24] The way we know and experience and become a person comes about as the result of an encounter between us and God in which 'objective and subjective elements are inextricably intertwined.'[25] Our raw human experience needs some framework for understanding and perceiving life. We interpret or understand new experiences in the context of earlier experiences and by building on these we form our personal history and story.[26] Schillebeeckx, another philosopher and theologian, suggests that the history of experience that forms our interpretative horizon also needs to keep us open to new experiences. Like Schillebeeckx, I live in this tension of exploring personhood in the light of God's revelation in me and in his Word. This makes the experience of living one of dynamic importance. As I struggled to understand why certain painful situations had happened to me, I can see now that I was 'blinded' by my emotions to the depths and wisdom found in Christ, God's Word. Yet this on its own was not sufficient to make sense of my experience. I needed my anger, my pain and my rejection to drive me on into a fresh discovery and encounter with God. I needed that objectivity of God but it also needed to become part of my subjective story, the story of my life.[27] I learnt that God's story was part of my story but I needed to look back with more scrutiny at events and experiences and see how the two stories met and merged.

Before reaching this understanding I felt that my life had to fit into a predetermined framework. Some of the depressing experiences I had been through, such as that engendered by a crippling sense of powerlessness caused by living in tied accommodation and the Church's inability to face its double standards, gave me fresh insights into the powerlessness of God on a cross, a central part of God's story. This sheds light, like the sun shining on the broken pieces of a mirror fallen on the floor. Our story belongs to us, and the process of discovering who we are and how we reflect the creative love of God begins with identifying the pieces, that are reassembled to reflect light, image and relationship once more. We are able to choose to tell others about who we are and how we have become the all that we are. Part of the potentially exciting and liberating experience of life is the discovery of our own unique story as we reflect and explore life and the way God has shaped it, for good or ill and usually both.

God shows us what he is like and involves himself in our story. The Bible begins by God saying, 'Let me tell you a story. In the beginning God'. What a great opening line but is this going to be a good story? Well, that is not a fair question because we know what happened next. It is like reading a whodunit murder mystery knowing who the culprit is before we start. There is a murder involved in the story of God. Rather than this being traumatic memory,

> Narrative theology affirms that God meets us in history, and . . . declares that God really became involved in our world of space and time, that God really entered into history, that God really came to meet us where we are. Often systematic theology creates the impression that God has presented us with a set of ideas, as if revelation were some kind of data bank. Narrative theology enables us to recover the central insight that God became involved in our history. God's story intersects with our story. We can understand our story by relating it to the story of God, as we read it in Scripture.[28]

One aspect of a psychodynamic theology is that it tells us what God is like through stories, rather than through a series of abstract, doctrinal propositions, although these stories may contain truths that need to be applied in their own way. The Old Testament is a telling of the story of God's love in creating a special people and how they struggled, worked and worshipped together, complete with adultery, battles, betrayal, healings, miracles, rebellion, spies, building projects and so on. Similarly the New Testament, especially the Gospels focused on Christ, is a story of God's love in repairing a broken relationship and the extending of this special relationship to all people, centering around the all-too-brief life, gruesome death and miraculous resurrection of Jesus. Paul and later writers shape their thinking around this story and the Bible concludes with a vision of God's love expressed in a future new creation with new bodies, a new heaven, a new earth and a timeless eternity of worship. God's story thus has a beginning, a middle and an end with the possibility of it being 'happy ever after'. An exciting feature of narrative theology is the possibility of the interplay, the interrelationship between God's story and our story. In the past we may have felt insignificant in the wider picture of what God was doing in his world, and the purpose of our lives was to 'fit in' with what we learnt about God and do his will. Narrative theology makes known to us knowledge about God and about ourselves that emerges out of the living, evolving story, rather than treating the story as a set of pre-planned, stage-managed moves. The difference is like the difference between playing in a football match chasing, tackling, passing, getting exhausted and soaking in the atmosphere and watching the edited highlights that appear on television. One is comfortable, the other is not, especially if it rains. One demands fifty per cent concentration, as they always show the goals again. The other demands one hundred per cent concentration, one blink and you've missed the tackle or the goal. One soothes and can be switched to another channel if the match is boring, the other growls, roars, jumps with elation or slumps with disappointment. One costs little, the other costs a great deal. Both are true representations of the football match but they need to be held together. One stresses objectivity and analysis, the other stresses participation, experience and subjectivity, but both are true. This concept is so important that I want to add a further analogy. Evelyn Glennie is one of the world's leading percussionists. She brandishes one or two rubber mallets, striking them against irregularly shaped pieces of wood or metal with the speed and accuracy of a Formula One driver. The surfaces resonate, vibrate and communicate sound – to some, but not to Glennie. She is deaf and can hear nothing. Words as sound do not exist but sound as vibration gives her a 'feel' for the music she is playing. What her eye sees as a certain musical note her ears and body register as a certain type of vibration, enabling her to produce highly creative percussion. Narrative theology is another way of discovering God; it can be highly creative and this creativity can be discovered both in theological and psychological terms.

Any theology that engages with people today requires a dynamism that communicates real truth and brings about relationship in a way people can understand; often they can best begin to understand their own lives and experience. David Lyall, a Scottish pastoral theologian, writing about pastoral counselling comments that,

> A major pastoral task is to assist counselees to talk concretely about themselves and to discover some of the symbols, stories

and myths of their lives . . . Narrative theology is concerned
to find personal meaning in stories and in the insights arising
from them [thus] . . . enabling people to understand the
stories of their own lives . . .There is no better library for
understanding people than the 'living human documents' of
people in crises . . . the one seeking counselling comes asking
for a fresh interpretation of what has been experienced, a
new 'story' for his or her life . . . yet the pastoral counsellor
is . . . also the bearer of stories and a Story.[29]

Enabling people to make connections within their life stories and
discover the intense relationality of God is a vital task. This is real
'dirt on the hands' theology, a theology that is truly practical.[30]
Yet any psychodynamic theology must also recognise the story-
telling and story-listening aspect of a therapeutic relationship. One
psychodynamic therapist Stephen Holmes describes his work.

The client in counselling tells a *story* – the clinical story is a
mixture of history, affect, assumption, recollection and
imagination conveyed as verbal and non-verbal communication. The story may be elaborated or sparse, muddled or
crystal-clear, riveting or boring, moving or flat – all of which
conveys meaning . . .The counselling hour is a fragment of
life comprising thousands of days and hundreds of thousands
of hours, yet a consistent pattern or thread runs through
them informing the way a client tells her story . . .The history
we tell reveals the meanings we live by . . .The process of
counselling can be seen as a recovery of a lost narrative –
of the client's life story.[31]

The lost narrative goes back into that lost relationship with God,
who is Persons in relationship and who calls us to be persons on
the way, with the hope of ultimate transformation. Our story
intersects with his story in a way that completes and fulfils his
purposes, brings us into wholeness and enables us to enter into
the stories of others with a new story to tell. The therapeutic
world is full of the stories of others, being told and re-told in a
manner which values and affirms them. Yet not everyone needs

a therapist to tell the story or make sense of it. Brian Keenan in the isolation of a Beirut captivity reflects,

> During my captivity I . . . was forced to confront the man I thought I was and to discover that I was many people. I had to befriend these many people, discover their origins, introduce them to each other and find a communality between themselves and myself . . . all our lives are but a story, and this is only another. Stories should be a mirror held up to life. Sometimes mirrors are cracked or opaque. Only those who look into it can truly know: you the reader will decide.[32]

What a psychodynamic theology provides is a meeting place in story. The narrative aspect of psychodynamic theology provides the ultimate context for our story, the psychological aspect of psychodynamic theology provides the means to help us identify the key relationships in a person's story. This psychodynamic view of personhood gives us a mechanism or a theoretical framework to help clarify the important roles others have played, or not played, in a person's life.

The challenging and exciting task in which I engage, as I write, preach and teach, enter into relationships, continue to be involved in counselling, is to see how our story is a true means of discovering knowledge about God and that it has a place in the continuing story of God. If we do not pass the God story on and demonstrate that the God story is true as an explanation of life, with its multi-faceted experiences and questions and as a resource to enable us to live fully, then it ceases to be. God will still be God, but his story will not be heard, to the impoverishment of all, and it will be incomplete. In one sense, we are participants in the writing of the end of the story.

We have explored two sides of the map, God as Persons in relationship and the story of God engaging with the story of our lives. My experience of therapy was that as I became able to relate to Tony in a new way – more openly, less guardedly, acknowledging my vulnerability and pain, my defences and my denials – I was more authentically human and more authentically theological in my thinking and feeling. As I came to see how vital my story was and the way it had shaped me, I saw that this had given me insights into others I could not have obtained any other way. Theology, spirituality, faith, counselling, psychology and psycho-dynamic insights all combined in a creative, life-affirming, God-glorifying way.

10

THE JOURNEY ON

I accepted the invitation to the new church believing that this was the 'right' step to take. The job seemed to fit me and my range of skills. The timing was good and the church was willing to allow me time to pursue my research degree, as well as to use my skills as a pastoral counsellor. The bad news was that the accommodation they had on offer was a two-bedroom bungalow which, while it suited a family with one child, gave no room for others or for family or guests to stay. This was to be the start of a painful saga where yet again we were let down by the church. On the one hand the church was very good, on the other it permitted things to happen to us that the members would not tolerate themselves. The bungalow needed gutting but as the church had run out of money they did all the work themselves. Despite some people working very hard, this still took nearly a year to complete. A promise had been made that the bungalow would be developed in two phases, the second to extend it and provide the necessary additional bedroom. We knew this would never happen but it was still a promise made to us that was never publicly referred to again or fulfilled. What was galling was that when emergency work was required for the church roof, the money was found. This of course is not a new event – many clergy, especially in the Free Church denominations, find themselves in housing that many church members would not be willing to live in. What it did was to uncover a deeply embedded strand in me that hated being power-less, alongside the emotional wounds I was still carrying from the accusations of the minister whose church I had tried to help.

After I had been at the church for four years, I saw a job

advertised that I thought would suit the academic and counselling skills that I had further developed. Despite being shortlisted, I did not get the job. Intriguingly, I now work as a tutor in pastoral counselling as part of an extension studies department with the person who did get the job. Ruth has become a friend and it has struck me how, in the purposes of God, some kind of circle was completed when this happened. I also think that Ruth has done a better job than I could. At the time it was disappointing as my spiritual journal for this period recalls. Yet it was more than that, it was unsettling. Without particularly wanting to move on from this church, I now became rather unrooted, like a tree shaken by a severe storm. I began to think about the future. There was one issue about which I was sure – that wherever I went I needed to believe that they would value me and my family needs and that, as far as I was concerned, meant the provision of proper housing. However, as various church options presented themselves, it seemed to me that the only way I could meet this need was to find a job either as a chaplain or in a community-based mental health team. I had interviews for both these jobs and again felt depressed when I was rejected. This led to a repeated experience of frustration and questioning, especially when some of the churches I was in contact with had, I discovered, either written me off as 'a liberal' because I had described my theological position as a critical, reflective evangelical or thought me 'unspiritual' because I was upfront about financial needs and the possibility of home ownership.

There was a roughness and pain about this time, like a wound that was continually being infected before it began to heal. Yet it was a productive time in ministry as I helped form a new congregation, saw answers to prayer (for others rather than myself) and was generally a 'good enough' church leader, although my colleague would say that I was not perhaps the easiest person to work with.

At long last though a church became available in the best geographical location possible, where I felt really at home; its potential excited me and the members were willing to look at housing because the previous minister owned his own home. I met with the elders and deacons and they brought a unanimous recommendation to the church that I become their next minister. Every criterion for guidance that I had used in the past indicated that this was just the right place for me to continue to fulfil my calling to lead in the Church. It was not to be, as I did not get the required majority of people voting for me to be invited as the next minister. It was reported back to me that some felt the financial demands on the church would be too great and others felt that I was not 'spiritual enough'. Spiritually, I had a sense of everything falling apart, so much so that I wanted to leave pastoral ministry. I experienced what can only be described as a period of spiritual depression. There was an overwhelming spiritual sadness dominated by a sense of God's absence when presence had been the normal experience. There was also a frightening sense of loss of my understanding of faith, as well as a frustrated powerlessness and loneliness. Others have described their experience this way, 'The inner loneliness arises out of a paradox: that in us which impels us to form relationships is, it seems, destined forever to be lonely.'[1] This is echoed by Nouwen in his chapter entitled 'Ministry by a Lonely Minister. The Wounded Healer'.

> He must bind his own wounds carefully in anticipation of the moment when he will be needed. He is called to be the wounded healer, the one who must look after his own wounds but at the same time be prepared to heal the wounds of others . . . But what are these wounds? . . . Maybe the word 'loneliness' best expresses our immediate experience and therefore most fittingly enables us to understand our brokenness. The loneliness of the minister is especially painful.[2]

How did this experience enable my theological and psychological reflections? We saw earlier that the north side of the map was an understanding of God as Persons in communion and therefore the source of all authentic relationship brought to us first in our early relationships. We can discover authentic relations through revelation which has an objective form, given in the words of Scripture and a narrative form found in the lives and stories of God's people, in us and in those we listen to. Having explored the north and south boundaries of the sketch map, we move now to the eastern edge which describes God as paradox. Yet theology does not have a monopoly on the experience of paradox. I remember an occasion when I sat in a rather plastic fast food outlet with tears rolling down my cheeks. I was embarrassed, not so much at being upset, but at being upset in such a tacky, inauthentic place. The cause of this display of emotion was having read a chapter of Nina Coltart's book *How to Survive as a Psychotherapist* where she describes the suicide of a client and her feelings about this. Her feelings deeply touched me and provoked an unexpected depth of emotion, where my tender recognition of such a sad loss and her surviving pain was in unspeaking yet articulate tears. Nina then discusses the issue of paradox.

> Not only does paradox turn up everywhere in how we live and work, but if we do not see and fully accept it, we deprive ourselves of a whole dimension of enjoyment, and – I think – skill . . . Seeking out, spotting, and tolerating paradoxes is essential to our peace of mind . . . We approach the paradox at the heart of the matter: psychotherapists are trained from their weaknesses; all other professions build on their strength.[3]

This resonated with much I have encountered in my spiritual and therapeutic journey. In my spiritual depression after a series of rejections and the seeming loss of a future, I entered into a fresh and intensely fragile relationship with God when I began to see that paradox is a theological as well as a life issue. One theologian, von Balthasar, amongst many others has struggled with this question when he wrote about the unknown God: 'It is no easy task to find one's way back from the "all too familiar" God to the truly unknown God.'[4] 'Does God cease to be when he reveals himself in His Son, to be the wholly other, the incomprehensible and crucified in Jesus of Nazareth, does he then come within reach of men?'[5] Yet it is precisely because the unknown, wholly other God enters into the chaos of the history of humanity that we discover the incomprehensible love of God. 'God . . . the ground of the absolute divine love outstrips immeasurably all human thought.'[6] Christians today must be capable of withstanding the tension which is contained within these statements. On one hand they must abandon every attempt to penetrate into the hidden and free being of God . . . and on the other hand they may reject a path which God offers . . . into the mystery of his eternal love. They may neither push God away into a realm of inaccessible transcendence . . . nor on the other hand so draw him into the historicity of the world that he forfeits his freedom over the world and falls victim to human *gnosis*.[7]

If God were not paradoxical, von Balthasar's and my fears would be realised. God would be reduced to a mere human knowing and subject to the whim and fancy of human intellect. People would become gods, and history, like some pockmarked, mine-ridden battle zone, is littered with the remains of those who have tried to be like God. None has been able to defeat death. Yet humanity continues its quest for immortality, ignorant of the offer given by God in Christ, made real to us by the Spirit of God today. In one sense these words can be seen as a particularly complex move on a theological chessboard. Yet my intellectual and internal worlds needed to find a meeting place, a safe haven, and discovering the paradox of God has enabled me to think and feel in a more integrated and unified way.

Paradox then is central to Christian faith and during this time it became a much more fully developed aspect of my own faith. If I had been able to know the future, to control people and events like some omniscient, omnipotent deity, I would have saved myself the pain and rejection of that wilderness time. Yet spiritually and psychologically I would be impoverished and less able to enter into the ravaged and damaged lives of others, with memories of my own scars and wounds, some healed and some still in the slow process of repair. Nouwen takes up this theme again.

Making one's own wounds a source of healing, therefore, does not call for a sharing of superficial personal pains but a constant willingness to see one's own pain . . . as arising from the depth of the human condition . . . How does this healing take place? Many words, such as care and compassion, under-standing and forgiveness, fellowship and community, have been used . . . I like to use the word hospitality . . . because it gives more insight into the nature of response to the human condition of loneliness.[8]

Yet paradoxically – the abyss of potential disintegration and darkness becomes a place to offer hospitality, companionship, friendship, tenderness and love. We can use Jim Cotter's phrase to become 'pain-bearers'.[9] One of the most genuinely Christian and humanly demanding tasks I did, even in this time of spiritual depression, was for my GP, who was also a friend. Carol did not have a particular faith yet respected those who did. When her son Peter was stillborn, Carol and her partner asked if I would take the funeral as I was one of the few religious people that they trusted. In this service I acknowledged their huge loss and I expressed my faith, which given the circumstances felt a great honour. Paradoxically death became the acknowledgement of life – a life lived in the womb – and an ongoing spiritual life. At the funeral the music played was Fauré's *Requiem*, described as a lullaby of death, and when I listen to this it brings back both the emotion and the wholeness of this event. Paradoxically the 'good enough' pastoral care I offered as a 'pain-bearer' happened outside the church community.

The overwhelming experience of darkness and absence of God can also be the very place where we encounter God, having been stripped of aspects of self and faith that have become superficial. This is the abyss of love I mentioned in chapter 6. My feelings then were similar to those described by Teilhard de Chardin.

> I allowed my consciousness to sweep back to the farthest limit . . . I stepped down into the most hidden depths of my being . . . in the blackest recesses of the blackness within me . . . with terror and intoxicating emotion, I realised that my own poor trifling existence was one with the immensity of all that is and all that is still in the process of becoming.[10]

In my theological and therapeutic roles I have encountered this theme again and again as I have explored the dimensions of people often hidden and only brought to light by the entering in of God in weakness, vulnerability and love. As I have sat with countless persons listening to their stories, staying in their darkness, feeling

138

their pain and nursing my own at the same time, I have been modelling the presence of God in their experience of the apparent absence of God.[11] Paradox is at the heart of life and the heart of God. Yet it is a word seemingly absent from my evangelical tradition, that is certain of its certainties and dubious about its doubts. Real theology for real people needs the recognition of real paradox. 'We students of God, look at us: God's own image scratching our eczema'; complaining about PMT, yet capable of reflecting divine glory and goodness; Homo sapiens, an evolved species who dream of eternity; playing God with the lives of others, yet ignorant of basic philosophy and believing in aliens; we are curious about heaven and hell but less so than about our star sign or winning the lottery; 'recipients of rationality who cannot balance our bank accounts; living souls puzzled by death'; aware of Aids but addicted to unprotected orgasm; such a being it is that puts fingers to keyboard and produces 'vague sentences about God; who breathes polluted air and speaks of Spirit' the very breath of God. 'It is because humanity is a paradox that the human study of God is and remains a paradox.'[12] If God is paradoxical, as I am suggesting he is, then we his people are also paradoxical. My psychodynamic theology recognises this, as do psychotherapists, and if the Church were able to acknowledge this to a greater degree, it might become more adult and mature.

The fourth and final western edge to our sketch map of buried treasure and a way of discovering the process of becoming is exploring how we understand God and ourselves, paradoxical as he is and we are, by using metaphorical language. McFague writes, 'a metaphor is seeing one thing as something else, pretending "this" is "that" because we do not know how to think or talk about "this" so we use "that" as a way of saying something about it.'[13] Thinking metaphorically means spotting a thread of similarity between two dissimilar objects or events. Jeremy Clarkson, a TV presenter and motoring journalist, uses both metaphor and analogy in a highly original way in his reports. 'If God is a Porsche, then the Devil is a Ferrari' is the kind of thing he might say. This metaphor implies that God is efficient, reliable, well-engineered, expensive, desirable but somehow lacking something. The kind of car you buy through a rational decision. The Devil is red, sexy, curvaceous, dangerous, head-turning and utterly desirable. The kind of car you buy through an emotional decision.

One view of Jesus Christ is that he himself is 'a parable of God' where we have no alternative but to recognise personal relational language as the most appropriate language about God.

> He was a person relating to other persons in loving service and transforming power. Poets use metaphor all the time because they are constantly speaking about the great unknowns – mortality, love . . . and so on. Religious language is deeply metaphorical . . . and it is no surprise that Jesus' most characteristic form of teaching, the parables, should be extended metaphors. We find in Scripture naturalistic, impersonal images balancing the relational, personal ones; God as rock, fortress . . . and so on. A metaphorical theology will insist that many metaphors and models are necessary, that a piling up of images is essential . . . to attempt to express the richness and variety of the divine human relationship.[14]

So as I sit with clients listening to their stories, I understand their struggles for companionship, friendship and belonging. I can see God coming to meet them as in the parable of the Prodigal Son. Wanting them, longing for them to come home. Yet as I listen and share in their story and offer a relationship, a sense of communion that springs from the life of the Trinitarian God in me, I hold in tension the objective revelation of God and his story and their need to discover real groundedness, real light in the abyss, real love – all of which can be found in God, metaphorically understood as a father or mother, a friend.

In the darkness and spiritual sadness I experienced when all that I had believed seem to fall apart like some flimsy toy that never survives longer than Christmas Day, it was through a loving and supportive wife and friends that God met with me again. By this stage I had left therapy, sensing that the time had come for me to be authentically me, on my own. I was adult enough, though still carrying a vulnerable child within, to face the powerlessness and unknownness of the future. Intriguingly, two of the three books I had written at that stage were *Helping the Depressed* and *Understanding Friends*.[15] I was sustained, held by a network of believing friends who not only believed in God, but crucially also believed in me. They did not give me glib answers, quote Bible verses or try and avoid the pain and rejection that I was experiencing. They enabled me to begin to see that God was also a friend. What they could offer to me, I began to see God could also offer me. My view of God was helped then by the metaphor of friend, although I still paradoxically hold onto the otherness of God. The theologian, Karl Barth, describes it this way.

> In being gracious to man in Jesus Christ, He also goes into the far country into the evil society of this being which is not God and against God. He does not shrink from him. He does not pass by ... God shows himself to be the great and true God in the fact that He can and will let his grace bear this cost, that he is capable and willing and ready for this condescension, this act of extravagance, this far country. What marks God out above all false gods is that they are not capable and willing and ready for this ...There can be no doubt about the full and genuine and individual humanity of the man Jesus of Nazareth; but in that man there has entered in and there must be recognised and respected One who is qualitatively different from all other men. He is not simply a ... greater man. But ... we have here in the person of this man One who is their Lord ... who has full power ... to pronounce in His existence a final word concerning them and all human history. He is the Saviour before whom there was none other, neither shall be after.[16]

The salvation I experienced at the age of fifteen, prepared by psychological conflict, is in the One whom Barth has described here. I did not meet him metaphorically then, I encountered the living, saving Lord. So my story with its psychological component, met, intersected with the story of God as an objective event in history. As my story has progressed, as I try to put flesh on the bones of Christian faith and as I have encountered others, a metaphorical theological understanding of God has been a helpful partner in knowing God and being known by God.

The use of metaphor is crucial to counselling and psychotherapy. A particular metaphor that I instinctively respond to is that of 'space'. Perhaps that stems from my fight for my own space from the moment of conception in being a twin. Psychodynamic writers such as Winnicott, Pruyser and Jacobs all discuss the notion of the transitional sphere or space as the place between our internal and external worlds which is creative, imaginative and pleasurable.[17] This space is a further development from a transitional object that 'is a transcendent, mysterious, symbolic object'. It gives access to 'the world of play, the world of imagination, the world of illusion' which opens up 'the options for growth and development'.[18] Transitional objects 'prefigure transcendent objects . . . charged with symbolic meaning, and lie at the heart of the visual arts, literature, the sciences, and religion and music.'[19] Pruyser writes autobiographically about the importance of symbol[20] in his own religious life and the changes in beliefs and values that he encountered.[21] This 'world' then is of crucial importance as it forms the arena in which beliefs and values are owned by the person through symbol and space. Our lives, theologically and therapeutically, are the places we encounter God and others. There is always the possibility of God breaking in or revealing himself[22] in a way that resonates with the experience of our internal world. This takes place in the transitional space. I can say that 'I believe in God and that God believes in me' and this 'genuinely is to speak of oneself from the heart, to reveal who one is by confessing one's essential belief, the faith that makes life worth living'.[23] Christian faith 'has its external source in God's self-disclosure, whose record is Scripture as . . . remembered by the living tradition, and its internal source in faith personally experienced.'[24] Here a person's life becomes the transitional space, as an encounter with God is not a sign of pathological dependence, but a radically new interdependence and where our internal and external worlds co-exist in a creative way that brings meaning to life.

Psychotherapists are involved in the perpetual quest to find language to describe what happens in this place of therapeutic encounter. While the notion of transitional sphere or space has been subjected to philosophical scrutiny and felt to be too general a term,[25] it is in a metaphorical sense that it has its greatest significance. I asked my son Toby (aged 7), in a pretend game of

Mastermind, what he liked best about his daddy. Toby replied 'Taking me to the park.' The park in question is a five-minute walk away from our house where on any possible pretext Toby drags me along so he can ride his bike. In the park there is a large, fenced children's play-area, with swings, seats, tarmac paths and grass hummocks. My sole function is to take Toby there and once there I sit and read a book – much to the amusement of some of the other parents – while he races around. Why does Toby enjoy this so much? My conclusion was that in this fenced area, with me in the vicinity, he has the space to explore, risk, run, do whatever he wants, become whomever he wants and meet whom he chooses, in a safe and bounded way. I have an important part to play in bringing Toby to this space and making it safe for him to explore, dream, and imagine as he wishes. Psychotherapy is like that. It needs safety, space, boundaries that are not always easy to identify but are obvious when they are there. Part of my desire to write a psychodynamic theology is to provide a theoretical way of forming some boundaries within which people can more truly experience themselves and God.

What issues does this raise for the Church of which I am part? Firstly, the challenge is to engage significantly with the story of God. So often it has been reduced to a set of simple formulae that caricature the immensity, grandeur and glory of God. There is an objective revelation in Scripture, but this needs to be engaged with, lived out, talked about, reflected on so that it introduces us again and again to the Living God. There are huge dangers for the Church in settling for an infant-like dependent relationship with God, where no one must make loud noises in case it wakes the children and they start crying. We are in danger of settling for a sanitised, Disney, 'happy ever after' cartoon version of the 'far country' rather than engaging in the hard and hazardous journey for ourselves and others. We want to define other people's space for them rather than take the risk of letting them discover that space for themselves.

Secondly, the challenge is to engage in real relationships with people and, if required, become pain-bearers. The qualities of a 'real' relationship are found in Jesus. The sheer power of his personhood is seen in his loving, accepting, healing, forgiving, risking, trusting, identifying with, listening to, sharing in, challenging, serving and dying. The death of self and the slaying of selfishness are at the heart of Christian believing. Yet that means paradoxically discovering who one's self really is. It means taking an inner journey, guided by a friend, a spiritual director, counsellor or psychotherapist. I have been helped by each of these people, greatly adding to the richness and diversity of my journey. The world is teeming with people in 'a far country' like lemmings on a march, heedless of the dangers ahead. Real relationship means getting alongside in an authentic way. Tragically the Church keeps its saints holy by keeping them in the 'safe' environment of a Christian community, like some sterile white hospital room designed to keep infections out. Jesus spoke powerfully about spiritual priorities when he called all to follow him in a pain-bearing brokenness of personhood, yet restored relationship with God where the choice was between the world and the soul (Matt. 16:26). Are we so concerned to preserve the soul at the expense of the world? Another paradox of faith is how the utterly holy, transcendent God gives of himself to become part of the struggle of each person to rid themselves of their alienation, contradictions and unholiness.

The situations I have encountered and the people I have experienced have led me on a journey into the depths of theology and psychology, in order to find some orientation and direction, initially for myself and now for others. This psychodynamic theology is but an embryonic step into a 'no-person's' land, taking the risk of leaving secure boundaries behind, in order to rescue the wounded and take them home, a home that has psychological and spiritual dimensions.

11

THE QUIET STORM

The sound increased from a dull throb to a rolling thunder as we walked up through the gorge, reaching the summit where a cascading waterfall was revealed. Here was life, water flowing, clean, alive, urgent in its path to beyond. The senses were invigorated; bodies ached, knees creaked, the heart slowed from its pumping of much needed oxygen, the breathing settled, the muscles relaxed as we stopped. This was our destination and now was the time for rest. The rest was short-lived however – for as the day moved on so must we, in order to be home by night. This chapter marks such a resting place. I can trace back the route we have come. I have taken the risk of entering that no-person's land, at the boundaries of faith and psychology, to offer a psychodynamic theology that engages with the deepest aspects of people. These risks are ones that push me to the boundaries of evangelical faith and my fear is that some will not be happy until I (and others like me), thinking, questioning and struggling, are pushed out altogether or put into exile. If that happens, then who will address the deep needs of so many people that are encountered when pain, depression, disillusionment or aloneness strip away the defences we use to contain our vulnerability? Who will speak for those in the Evangelical Church that are silenced by fear of rejection? The theological dynamics I offer have a number of distinct features that I have discovered in my own story, which, I hope, will become part of the stories of others and give a voice to the speechless, those rendered mute by their pain. The risk, in developing this psychodynamic theology, is one of becoming a lone voice crying in the wilderness, yet my instincts tell me that there are many who will hear it with recognition and relief.

Firstly, I have sought to be both biblical and radical in a way that offers a life-giving and life-affirming hope. Secondly, I have sought to demonstrate a depth and integrity that encounter real pain – our own, and others. Thirdly, I have become a temporary guide to take people on a journey of faith in the rediscovery of their personhood by engaging their story or narrative in a new way. This story values both the individual – what it is to 'be' for self, and the community – and what it is to 'be' for others. Fourthly, I have celebrated the being and uniqueness of what it is to be a person. This also requires us to acknowledge our own vulnerability and weakness, as well as the contingency of our thinking. Fifthly, I have roughed out a sketch map to chart spiritual and therapeutic 'space' where I can encounter self, God and others.

As I look at myself and the person I am on the way to becoming, there are biblical characters who resonate with me. They make sense for me here and now, rather than being quaint, old, dusty characters whose exploits one heard about in Sunday school. I cannot claim to be them. I do not have Joseph's administrative or interpretative abilities, David's fighting or poetic abilities, Samson's strength or hair, Ezekiel's ecstatic experiences or Jeremiah's depressions. To claim these would be audacious and I would never want to be the clone of another. Yet I can see things in them that I sense also within myself.

As I was writing a series of sermons on the early chapters of Isaiah, I came to chapter six and Isaiah's supernatural experience of seeing and encountering God. This passage gave me a succinct portrait of the prophet, that also brought fresh insights to me. He was someone with an immense vision of God. My vision of my awesome God has been renewed as I have grappled again with the transcendence of the One who is the source of all being, life, love, hope and wholeness. Yet Isaiah resonates with me too because in the later chapters we see Christ prefigured in the suffering servant who becomes immanent in incarnation and identification with the most profound pain. Whatever our pain is, there is one who has entered into that abyss, in identification and in reparation. Post-modern pain, it seems to me, is a disconnection with anything rooted or authentic. The existential inner loneliness that Moore[1] talks of has become the post-modern way of life. Our culture is floundering for someone big enough to believe in. The radicalness of truly taking on board the implications of a triune God is that there is no one bigger. Even the psychological language I have used to describe personhood is but a whisper of the transcendent God. God is Person, authentic being, source and end of all.

Isaiah was also someone deeply aware of his own sinfulness. My sinfulness is real and I have not tried to hide it in these pages. I do not think I am irredeemably sinful, in the gut-wrenching, guilt-inducing way which once characterised certain Reformed and fundamentalist Christian traditions, with their lists of wrongdoing. Sin, it has been said, is a powerful metaphor of what sits between us and God. In our fear of intimacy with God we hold onto the world we have created for ourselves, which excludes God. Part of us desperately desires God and yet another part of us is afraid. Afraid to let go, like a child clinging to its mother not yet sure whether it is safe to reach out and take the sweet proffered in the outstretched hand of the giver. Sin stays with us as we still in adulthood stubbornly cling to doing it our way, getting on with our life, with little reference and no accountability to any other. Isaiah lived at a time when the people, God's very special chosen people, were doing it their way and how God detested them and what they had become with their pride and pseudo-spirituality. Yet Isaiah begins by acknowledging his own fear of intimacy with God, as it exposes him at his most vulnerable. I hate my vulnerability, yet paradoxically, it is when I acknowledge it, live with it and allow others to see it and share in it, that God works in bringing wholeness to others. For me sin would be to pretend I had everything together, to be the professional minister, the qualified pastoral counsellor, and the emerging pastoral theologian. I am these things in weakness, failure, with my need to belong, my insecurities, my lack of insight and my slothful spirituality.

Isaiah was a person who had a profound experience of the grace and the goodness of God. God met him, and his faith, which would sustain him in times of ridicule and rejection, arose out of this searing and purifying encounter with a gracious God, who drew him into intimate relationship and wholeness. God knowing everything about me – each thought, action, intention, reaction, emotion and longing (conscious and unconscious) – still acts in Christ's entering into the abyss of pain, non-being, suffering, disintegration, death and a splitting of the Trinity (Persons in communion) and becomes a non-person. Why? So that I can truly become the person God created me to be. I have the faintest glimmer of that as I sit sharing in the story of the client before me trying to reconcile the split aspects of the self they are discovering after years of emotional, physical and sexual abuse. Their aspects of self reach out to one another in such a tender, fragile way, where even to trust another with their story has taken years. Yet God comes to encounter me, dimly understanding, psychologically vulnerable and needy as a fifteen year old sitting in a church. That was my God event, paradoxically unlike and so like Isaiah's. No visions of angelic beings, thunder or smoke but rather a still, small voice calling in a way that I could hear. It is a voice that called into being a new spiritual being. I like Kovel's definition of spirituality which 'is the practical creation of the spirit, where spirit is what transpires when the self experiences a surpassing of its own boundedness and relates itself to a larger framework of being.'[2] The lyrics of the song *Quiet Storm* by Phil and John capture this experience, echoing as they do Barth's image of the 'far country'.

> I searched for truth in a far country
> It was there I found no peace at all
> I laid my head where the wisest men
> Where the wisest men would often fall
> As my ambition rode a roundabout
> And left me battered, bruised and worn
>
> Then in your love you rescued me
> Just like a quiet storm
>
> You saw beneath all my arguments
> It was easy then to see the truth
> You saw right through all this grand facade
> Now my peace of mind is found in you

As my emotions rode a roundabout
And then lay battered, bruised and torn

You clothed me in your righteousness
And breathed a quiet storm
You clothed me in your righteousness
And breathed a quiet storm
And when the night is dark and cold
And I have nowhere left to turn

Then let me know you'll stand by me
And be my quiet storm
Then let me know you'll stand by me
And be my quiet storm
And be my quiet storm[3]

Isaiah then stepped where I have not yet been able to step. He became willing to be spent in the service of God, whatever the cost. His mission was not quite, but nearly, impossible and he had no Hollywood multi-million dollar budget to help him either. Yet he gathered around himself a new school of prophets, a new group of followers, who formed a remnant that God was to use in incredible ways. Isaiah and I part company here, as I have no desire to gather a group of people around me doing anything as remotely dubious as prophecy. Yet, paradoxically, as I speak at conferences, engage with therapists, psychiatrists, theologians and just ordinary people like myself, I am discovering a searching and a yearning similar to my own. We may not be prophetic but I think the Church will need to come to hear our collective voice that God must be God, Person must be persons, refracted in us, albeit dimly, not in some static, life-denying way but in living, dynamic, risk-taking relationship. The cost is that authentic relationship needs time, nurture, love and care – and such resources are limited in the late twentieth century. The Church as a vibrant, worshipping community should be the place where our resources are renewed. Yet so often I feel my emotional energies are ravished by the incessant demands of needy Christians resisting attempts to nurture their psychological and spiritual growth. Like babies they resist the messy business of learning to feed themselves.

I am not sure how Isaiah encountered the metaphor of 'space' but he did see heaven and earth joined in his own emotional experience. My sense of 'space' allows me to become 'me' with my splits and shadow, my limited ability to forgive, my paradoxical intimacy and distance from God, my sense of aloneness and yet my completeness by those that love me. My 'space' is bigger now than it ever has been before, yet infinitely more vulnerable. I even question now the consequences of writing as honestly as I can in a way that opens me to the risk of being at the mercy of others. Yet this discovery of 'space' is a joyful celebration of life – a life not yet fully lived and longing to be lived. The evangelist in me longs to introduce others to this place of spiritual and psychological encounter. As a result of this 'space' I can be 'me' and being 'me' is of huge significance. I can therefore be of help to others, both as a minister and a counsellor, because I am able to 'be' and I can have faith in my 'being' as well as being in relationship with God. Isaiah's dream was to tell God's story and that is my dream; it alternates with another, to listen to the stories of others in a way that enables them to hear God's story because their own has been heard perhaps for the very first time.

My story has focused on my search for my own 'space'. This began at conception and continues still. Some of the experiences recounted here, often painful yet strangely exhilarating, have allowed me to discover the 'space' in me and others, including God. This 'space' enables the living communication of love, friendship, faith and care that I offer to those who encounter me as 'me', a minister or a therapist. This is a good place, a faith-enabling and psychodynamically-aware place, to reach on my journey. Yet it is only a resting place, the journey continues.

NOTES

Introduction

1. Bebbington (1989), pp. 249f.
2. Rose (1995), p. 54.

1: Family Matters

1. Details on Lake can be found in his *Clinical Theology* (1966) and my book *An Evaluation of Clinical Theology* (1994). Winnicott's work is more diverse but a helpful introduction and critique can be found in *Winnicott* by Jacobs (1995) and a helpful appreciation in Goldman (ed.), *In One's Bones* (1993). A good introduction to twins is Bryan's *Twins, Triplets and more* (1992). A psychodynamic understanding of twins can be found in my unpublished dissertation, 'The psychodynamics of twins – a theoretical exploration'.
2. See Jacobs' (1995) comments on Winnicott, p. 3.

2: Finding Faith

1. Gordon (1963).
2. Bray (1993), pp. 248–9.
3. Bainton (1978), p. 65.
4. If the Trinity as Father, Son and Holy Spirit, Creator, Redeemer and Sustainer is 'the distinctively Christian understanding of God' (Webster, 1995, p. 4) then I was, in practice, a Christocentric modalist keeping company with various well-known early church heretics (McGrath, 1994, pp. 256f.; Bray, 1993).
5. Lyric sheet from the Trilogy, part 3, *In Another Land* (Solid Rock Records).
6. Norman (1991), p. 20.

7. For a fascinating discussion of this see Ward (ed.), *Is Psychoanalysis another religion?* (1993).
8. See Magdalen (1994).
9. Hughes (1985), p. 10.

3: You'll Never Walk Alone

1. Fowler distinguishes faith from religion and belief. He sees faith as possessing four specific attributes, two of which are so fundamental to human existence, that I think they would generally be termed belief and values. He writes, 'Believing or beliefs can be important constituent parts of faith . . . but cannot be equated with faith. Belief tries to bring faith to expression. But faith is more than intellectual assent to propositions of dubious verifiability' (Hunter, 1990, pp. 394–5). He is trying to safeguard the word faith to mean a 'practical commitment that involves both conscious and unconscious aspects. It is a moral and existential orientation of the total self to that which has the value of sacred for a person or group' (p. 395). This is somewhat confusing but I understand his desire to make a distinction between a general intellectual belief, that may have little consequence for the living of life, and a specific life-involving belief, which he would term 'faith' that may have huge consequences for the living of life.
2. Fowler in 'Faith Development Research' in Hunter (1990), p. 400.
3. Ibid.
4. Ibid.
5. Fowler quoted in Bridger, 'Faith Development' in Atkinson and Field (1995), p. 370.
6. Fowler in 'Faith Development Research' in Hunter (1990), p. 401.
7. The strengths of Fowler's ideas are that: they offer an important model of human development drawing on acknowledged theories and empirical data; and, they attempt to integrate a theological understanding of faith with insights drawn from psychology. Fowler's work can be criticised for: the impression that a linear development of faith is the most important; a questioning of whether such stages can sufficiently cover the range of ideas presented by Erikson, Piaget and Kohlberg; an awareness that Fowler offers 'a phenomenogically useful but theologically inadequate definition of faith' (Bridger, 'Faith Development' in Atkinson, 1995, p. 371); a limited empirical base that fails to allow for cultural and gender differences; and an over emphasis on individual psychology at the expense of a wider social context. To some extent these failings are addressed by Michael Jacobs with his concept of 'living illusions' (see his book of the same name). He refines

Fowler's work by including Freud's developmental stages summarised as trust and dependency, authority and autonomy and cooperation and competition, before adding his own stage of complexity and simplicity and illustrating each stage from the work of Winnicott. He broadens Fowler's work by including theologians such as Tillich, Faber and Cupitt, although this is still a rather selective range.

8. See CTA 6–6 and Jacobs (1993).
9. Ibid.
10. See Brown and Pallant, pp. 282–3 and Stanley, pp. 345–350 in Brown (1973).
11. I am not alone in this. See Jo Ind (1993), Dave Tomlinson (1994) and Nigel Wright (1996).
12. See Atkinson (1991).
13. See Magdalen (1994).

4: The Good, the Bad and the Ugly

1. Rayner (1986), pp. 246–7.
2. Quoted in Ross (1994), section 6.5.1.
3. See Douglas (1995).
4. Skynner and Cleese (1983), pp. 276–280.
5. A simple model for theological reflection can be found in my article 'Stress and Theological Reflection', published in *Ministry Today* (October 1995).
6. von Balthasar (1990), p. 29.
7. Rayner (1986), pp. 152–4.

5: The Pain and Power of Ministry

1. This is a not uncommon pattern discussed by Kirk and Leary (1994), p. 39 and pp. 125–140.
2. Ibid., p. 16.
3. E. Pattison, 'Defence and Coping Theory' in R. Hunter (1990), pp. 267–9.
4. Jacobs (1982), pp. 93–4.
5. See Storkey (1995).
6. See A.H. Modell, ' "The Holding Environment" and the Therapeutic Action of Psychoanalysis' in Golman (1993), pp. 273–289.
7. Jacobs (1988), p. 82.
8. Jacobs (1982), p. 48.
9. Kirk and Leary (1994), p. 135.
10. See Green and Townsend (1994).

11. Michael Wilcock's treatment of Samson in *The Message of JUDGES* is an exception to this general trend.
12. Houston (1989), p. 6.
13. Schmidt (1995), pp. 7–8. Some would still find Schmidt's approach too condemning, despite the clear desire to be as helpful and caring as possible. The issue of homosexuality was helpfully discussed in *Third Way*, vol. 18. no. 10, Dec. 1995.
14. For a non-technical explanation of this see Skynner and Cleese (1983), pp. 253 and pp. 191–6. For the importance of triangular relationships see Jacobs (1986), pp. 96–7.
15. Freud, 'Postcript to "The Question of Lay Analysis"' in *Historical and Expository Works on Psychoanalysis*, vol. 15, The Pelican Freud Library (1986), p. 257.
16. Wright (1996).
17. NB Book Reviews, UCCF, December 1996.
18. See Tomlinson (1995).

6: Into the Abyss

1. du Maurier (1978), p. 16.
2. For a description and critique see the articles on 'inner healing' and 'prayer counselling' in Benner (1985) and Atkinson and Field (1995).
3. A more detailed account is contained in Ross (1990).
4. Symington (1986), pp. 30–1.
5. Skynner and Cleese (1983), pp. 17–20.
6. Alighieri, *Hell*, translated by Ellis (1995), p. 1.
7. See the index of *Clinical Theology*.
8. See Green and Townsend (1994), p. 2.
9. St John of the Cross, *Dark Night of the Soul*, translated by Peers (1976), p. 55.
10. Quoted in Atkinson (1991), pp. 30–1.
11. Lake (1966), p. 912.
12. McLeod (1987), p. 891.
13. See Brown (1978), p. 382.
14. Fox (1983).
15. Macquarrie (1966), p. 245.
16. Fox (1983), p. 135.
17. Ibid., pp. 141–2.
18. Ibid., pp. 144–5.
19. Ibid., pp. 153–4, 161.
20. Yalom (1989), pp. 35–6.
21. See Suttie's book of the same title.
22. Winnicott (1975), p. 195.
23. Keenan (1992), p. xiii.

8: Investigating the Institution

1. My theoretical knowledge consisted of Bion's *Experience in Groups*, De Board's *The Psychoanalysis of Organizations* and Reed's *The Dynamics of Religion*. This has expanded and now includes Freud (1985), Hinshelwood (1987), Lyth (1988), Obholzer and Roberts (1994) and Douglas (1995).
2. Honesty compels me to admit that there was one breach of confidence that I was responsible for. At the time it was to counter an unfair accusation about the group, but I wish it had not happened.
3. See Wright (1989).
4. Townsend (1996).
5. Howatch (1994), p. 216.
6. Bion (1961).
7. Reed (1978), p. 223.
8. Obholzer and Roberts (1994), pp. 22–3.
9. Reed (1978), p. 225.
10. For a theological discussion of evil see Wright (1989).
11. Atkinson (1991), p. 81.
12. I view myth as an engaging tradition-authenticated story dealing with the origin, nature and purpose of the world and its inhabitants. Often featuring divine beings, these stories are sometimes taken as true in a historical sense but psychologists and others tend to view them as creative imaginings that serve vital personal, social and religious functions.
13. See Jacobs (1992), p. 40.
14. Quoted in Jacobs (1992), p. 42.
15. Blocher (1984), p. 139.
16. Ibid., pp. 141–2.
17. Theissen (1987).
18. Obholzer and Roberts (1994), p. 12.
19. Lewis (1940).
20. Jacobs (1988) outlines why this is unhelpful.
21. See 'Persona and Shadow' in Chave-Jones (1989).
22. Quoted in Jacobs (1995), p. 81.
23. Obholzer and Roberts (1994), p. 12.

9: The Journey Within

1. Hobson (1985), p. 164.
2. Ibid., p. 173.
3. For a working definition see McGrath (1996), p. 22.
4. Hobson (1985), p. 173.
5. Ward and Wild (1995), pp. 2–3.

6. While there is an increasing flexibility about evangelical thinking, expressed by Wright (1996) and McGrath (1996), the experience of the people I meet is still that it can be controlling or punitive if questioned or challenged.

7. See Oden's *The Living God* (1987), *The Word of Life* (1989) and *Life in the Spirit* (1992).

8. For a lively exploration of this subject see Goldingay (1990), especially the chapters by Oliver and Atkinson.

9. Lake (1966) and my article 'The Dynamic Cycle' in Atkinson and Field (1995).

10. McFadyen quoted in Atkinson and Bridger (1994), p. 142.

11. Gunton (1993), p. 210.

12. Wright (1996), p. 14.

13. von Balthasar (1975), pp. 33–4.

14. Bowlby (1980), p. 442.

15. Atkinson (1994), p. 144.

16. I personally subscribe to the view that the primary motivational drive in people is to seek relationship, as a reflection of the image of God in each person. God in three persons exists in interrelationship and is always expressing being in love by giving. See also Suttie, *The Origins of Love and Hate* (1988) and Winnicott's (1965) brief discussion of theology, pp. 94–6.

17. A survey of these can be found in Wulff (1991), pp. 327–344.

18. A detailed psychodynamic developmental approach can be found in Rayner (1986).

19. 'New Introductory Lectures on Psychoanalysis', pp. 107–112.

20. Symington (1986) cautions that those involved in counselling may be too familiar with these terms and that Freud's understanding of the model of the mind is the most complex aspect of psychoanalytic theory, pp. 144–152.

21. Freud (1933), p. 105.

22. Jacobs (1988), pp. 9–10.

23. Brown and Pedder (1991), p. 51.

24. See the chapter 'The need for an objective form of revelation' in von Balthasar (1982), pp. 429f.

25. Ibid.

26. Quoted in Schreiter and Hilkert (1989), p. 37.

27. For a helpful discussion of narrative theology and revelation see R. Neibuhr's 'The Story of Our Life' found in Hauerwas and Jones (1989).

28. McGrath (1994), p. 173.

29. Lyall (1995), p. 101.

30. For a helpful introduction to practical theology see Ballard and Pritchard (1996).

31. J. Holmes, 'Attachment theory – a secure theoretical base for counselling?' *Psychodynamic Counselling*, vol. 1, no. 1, October 1994, p. 73.
32. Keenan (1992), pp. xiii–xv.

10: The Journey On

1. Moore (1982), p. 1.
2. Nouwen (1979), pp. 82f.
3. Coltart (1993), p. 39.
4. von Balthasar (1975), pp. 21f.
5. Ibid., p. 18.
6. Ibid.
7. Ibid., p. 25.
8. Nouwen (1979), pp. 88f.
9. Cotter (1993), pp. 49–56.
10. Quoted in McFague (1987), p. 4.
11. See Long (1990) for a very helpful exploration of the importance of listening.
12. All references Oden (1987), p. 405.
13. McFague (1982), p. 15.
14. McFague (1987), p. 20.
15. Sadly both are now out of print. Copies of *Understanding Friends* are available from the author.
16. Barth (1956), pp. 158–9.
17. Malloney (1991), p. 52.
18. Ibid., pp. 174–5.
19. Jacobs (1993), p. 143.
20. Lawson and McCauley (1993) develop another understanding and use of symbol in their cognitive approach to symbolic-cultural systems.
21. Malloney (1991), pp. 180–2.
22. God being traditionally defined as a plurality of persons.
23. Oden (1987), p. 11.
24. Ibid., p. 26.
25. Jacobs (1995), pp. 116–18.

11: The Quiet Storm

1. Moore (1982).
2. J. Kovel, 'The Meeting of Psychoanalysis and Religion' in Ward (1993), p. 19.
3. Used with the permission of the songwriter Phil Baggley.

REFERENCES

Alighieri, D., *Hell*, translated by S. Ellis (Vintage: London, 1995)

Atkinson, D., *The Message of Job* (IVP: Leicester, 1991)

Atkinson, D. and Bridger, F., *Counselling in Context* (HarperCollins: London, 1994)

Atkinson, D. and Field D. (eds.), *New Dictionary of Christian Ethics and Pastoral Theology* (IVP: Leicester, 1995)

Bainton, R., *Here I Stand* (Lion: Tring, 1978)

Ballard, P. and Pritchard, J., *Practical Theology in Action* (SPCK: London, 1996)

Barth, K., *Church Dogmatics* vol. 4., *The Doctrine of Reconciliation* (T&T Clark: Edinburgh, 1956. Translated and edited by G. Bromiley)

Balthasar, H. von, *Elucidations* (SPCK: London, 1975)

—— *The Glory of the Lord* (T&T Clark: Edinburgh, 1982)

—— *Credo. Meditations on the Apostles' Creed* (T&T Clark: Edinburgh, 1990)

Bebbington, D., *Evangelicalism in Modern Britain* (Unwin Hyman: London, 1989)

Bedford, C., *Weep for the City* (Lion: Tring, 1982)

Benner, D. (ed.), *Baker Dictionary of Psychology* (Baker Books: Grand Rapids, Michigan, 1985)

Bion, W., *Experience in Groups* (Tavistock: London, 1961)

Blocher, H., *In the Beginning* (IVP: Leicester, 1984)

Bloesch, D., *God the Almighty* (Paternoster: Carlisle, 1995)

Bowlby, J., *Attachment and Loss: Vol. 3* (Hogarth Press: London)

Bray, G., *The Doctrine of God* (IVP: Leicester, 1993)

Brown, C. (ed.), *New International Dictionary of New Testament Theology* (Zondervan: Grand Rapids, Michigan, 1978)

Brown, L. (ed.), *Psychology and Religion* (Pelican: Harmondsworth, 1973)

Bryan, E., *Twins, Triplets and more* (Penguin: Harmondsworth, 1992)

Berger, P. *et al.*, *The Homeless Mind* (Penguin Books: Harmondsworth, 1974)

Chave-Jones, M. *Listening to your feelings* (Lion: Oxford, 1989)

Cleese, J. and Skynner, R., *LIFE and how to survive it* (Methuen: London, 1993)

CTA, *Tutor's Manual* (CTA: Church Westcote, 1995)

Coltart, N., *How to Survive as a Psychotherapist* (Sheldon Press: London, 1993)

Cotter, J., *Pleasure, Pain and Passion*, second edn (Cairns Publications: Sheffield, 1993)

De Board, R., *The Psychoanalysis of Organizations* (Tavistock: London, 1978)

Douglas, T., *Survival in Groups* (Open University Press: Buckingham, 1995)

—— *Scapegoats. Transferring blame* (Routledge: London, 1995)

Erikson, E., *Young Man Luther* (Norton: New York, 1958)

Erikson, M., *Christian Theology* (Marshall Pickering: Basingstoke, 1987)

Fox, M., *Original Blessing* (Bear & Co.: Santa Fe, 1983)

Freud, S., *The Future of an Illusion*, revised edition (London, 1962)

—— *Civilization, Society and Religion*, vol. 12, The Pelican Freud Library (Penguin Books: Harmondsworth, 1985)

—— *Historical and Expository Works on Psychoanalysis*, vol. 15, The Pelican Freud Library (Penguin Books: Harmondsworth, 1986)

Goldman, D. (ed.), *In One's Bones. The Clinical Genius of Winnicott* (Aronson: New Jersey, 1993)

Goldingay, J. (ed.)., *Atonement Today* (SPCK: London, 1995)

Gordon, E., *Miracle on the River Kwai* (Hodder & Stoughton: London, 1963)

Green, M. and Townsend, A., *Hidden Treasure* (DLT: London 1994)

Gunton, C., *The One, The Three and The Many* (Cambridge University Press: Cambridge, 1993)

Hauerwas, S. and Jones, L.G., *Why Narrative? Readings in Narrative Theology* (Eerdmans: Grand Rapids, 1989)

Hinshelwood, R., *What happens in groups* (Free Association Books: London, 1987)

Hobson, R., *Forms of Feeling* (Tavistock: London, 1985)

Houston, J., *The Transforming Friendship* (Lion: Oxford, 1989)

Howatch, S., *Absolute Truths* (HarperCollins: London, 1994)

Hughes, G., *God of Surprises* (DLT: London, 1985)

Hunter, R. (ed.), *Dictionary of Pastoral Care and Counselling* (Abingdon: Nashville, TN, 1990)

Ind, J., *Fat is a spiritual issue* (Mowbray: London, 1993)

Jacobs, M., *Still Small Voice. An introduction to pastoral counselling* (SPCK: London, 1982)

—— *The Presenting Past* (Harper & Row: London, 1986)

—— *Psychodynamic Counselling in Action* (Sage: London, 1988)

—— *S. Freud* (Sage: London, 1992)

—— *Living Illusions* (SPCK: London, 1993)

—— *D.W. Winnicott* (Sage: London, 1995)

John of the Cross, St, *Dark Night of the Soul*, translated by E. Peers (Burns & Oates: Tunbridge Wells, 1976)

Keenan, B., *An Evil Cradling* (Hutchinson: London, 1992)

Kirk, M. and Leary, T., *Holy Matrimony* (Lion: Oxford, 1994)

Lake, F., *Clinical Theology* (DLT: London, 1966)

Lawson, E.T. and McCauley, R. *Rethinking Religion* (CUP, Cambridge, 1993)

Lewis, C.S., *The Problem of Pain* (Fontana: London, 1940)

Long, A., *Listening* (Daybreak/DLT: London, 1990)

Lyall, D., *Counselling in a pastoral and spiritual context* (OUP: Milton Keynes, 1994)

Lyth, I., *Containing Anxiety in Institutions* (Free Association Books: London, 1988)

McLeod, W. (ed.) *The New Collins Dictionary and Thesaurus* (Collins: London, 1987)

McFague, S., *Metaphorical Theology* (SCM: London, 1982)

—— *Models of God* (SCM: London, 1987)

McGrath, A., *Christian Theology* (Blackwell: Oxford, 1994)

—— *A passion for truth* (IVP: Leicester, 1996)

MacQuarrie, J., *Principles of Christian Theology* (SCM: London, 1966)

Magdalen, M., *The Hidden Face of Jesus* (DLT: London, 1994)

Malloney, H.N. (ed.), *Religion in Psychodynamic Perspective* (OUP: Oxford, 1991)

Maurier, D. du, *The Jamaica Inn* (Victor Gollancz: London, 1978)

Moore, S., *The Inner Loneliness* (DLT: London, 1982)

Norman, L., Lyric Sheet on the Album: *Only Visiting This Planet* (1972), p. 4

Nouwen, H., *The Wounded Healer* (DLT: London, 1979)

Obholzer, A. and Roberts, V., *The Unconscious at Work* (Routledge: London, 1994)

Oden, T., *The Living God* (HarperCollins: San Francisco, 1987)

—— *The Word of Life* (HarperCollins: San Francisco, 1989)

—— *Life in the Spirit* (HarperCollins: San Francisco, 1992)

Packer, J., *Knowing God* (Hodder & Stoughton: London, 1973)

Rayner, E., *Human Development*, third edition (Unwin Hyman: London, 1986)

Reed, B., *The Dynamics of Religion* (DLT: London, 1978)

Rose, G., *Love's Work* (Chatto & Windus: London, 1995)

Ross, J.A., *Helping the Depressed* (Kingsway: Eastbourne, 1990)

—— *Understanding Friends* (SPCK: London, 1993)

—— *An Evaluation of Clinical Theology* (CTA: Oxford, 1994)

Schmidt, T.E., *Straight and Narrow?* (IVP: Leicester, 1995)

Schreiter, R. and Hilkert, M., *The Praxis of Christian Experience* (Harper & Row: San Francisco, 1989)

Skynner, R. and Cleese, J., *Families and how to survive them* (Methuen: London, 1983)

Smith, N., *Winter Past. A story of depression and healing* (IVP: Leicester, 1978)

Snyder, H., *New Wineskins* (Marshall, Morgan & Scott: London, 1977)

Stevens, A., *On Jung* (Pelican: Harmondsworth, 1990)

Storkey, E., *The Search for Intimacy* (Hodder & Stoughton: London, 1995)

Suttie, I., *The Origins of Love and Hate* (Free Association Books: London, 1988)

Symington, N., *The Analytic Experience* (Free Association Books: London, 1986)

Theissen, G., *Psychological Aspects of Pauline Theology* (T&T Clark: Edinburgh, 1987)

Tomlinson, D., *The Post-Evangelical* (Triangle/SPCK: London, 1995)

Townsend, A., *Good Enough for God* (Triangle/SPCK: London, 1996)

Ward, I. (ed.), *Is Psychoanalysis another religion?* (Freud Museum Publications: London, 1993)

Webster, J., 'God' in D. Atkinson and D. Field (eds.), *New Dictionary of Christian Ethics and Pastoral Theology* (IVP: Leicester, 1995)

Wilcock, M., *The Message of JUDGES* (IVP: Leicester, 1992)

Winnicott, D.W., *Collected Papers* (Tavistock Publications: London, 1975 second edition)

Wright, N., *The fair face of evil* (Marshall Pickering: London, 1989)

—— *The Radical Evangelical* (SPCK: London, 1996)

Wulff, D., *Psychology of Religion* (Wiley: New York, 1991)

Yalom, I., *Love's Executioner* (Penguin: Harmondsworth, 1989)

INDEX

162